I AM A TOWN

I AM A TOWN

A COLLECTION OF STORIES BY SHARI SMITH

RIVER'S EDGE
—— MEDIA ——
Little Rock, Arkansas
2014

The author has tried to recreate events, locales and conversations from memories of them. In order to maintain anonymity, in some instances the names of individuals and places, some identifying characteristics and details such as physical properties, occupations and places of residence may have changed. The author and publisher do not assume and hereby disclaim any liability to any party for any loss or damage.

I AM A TOWN
by Shari Smith

Copyright © Shari Smith, 2014

www.RiversEdgeMedia.com

Published by River's Edge Media, LLC
100 Morgan Keegan Drive, Ste. 305
Little Rock, AR 72202

Edited by Judith Richards
Cover design by Cary A. Smith

Manufactured in the United States of America.
ISBN-13: 978-1-940595-10-8
Printed in the United States of America.

Lyrics of "I AM A TOWN"
Written by Mary Carpenter

Dedicated to the Boys at the Back Table and my father;
the best story tellers I know

I'm a town in Carolina, I'm a detour on a ride
For a phone call and a soda, I'm a blur from the driver's side
I'm the last gas for an hour if you're going twenty-five
I am Texaco and tobacco, I am dust you leave behind

I am peaches in September, and corn from a roadside stall
I'm the language of the natives, I'm a cadence and a drawl
I'm the pines behind the graveyard, and the cool beneath their shade, where
the boys have left their beer cans
I am weeds between the graves.

My porches sag and lean with old black men and children
Their sleep is filled with dreams, I never can fulfill them
I am a town.

I am a church beside the highway where the ditches never drain
I'm a Baptist like my daddy, and Jesus knows my name
I am memory and stillness, I am lonely in old age; I am not your destination
I am clinging to my ways
I am a town.

I'm a town in Carolina, I am billboards in the fields
I'm an old truck up on cinder blocks, missing all my wheels
I am Pabst Blue Ribbon, American, and "Southern Serves the South"
I am tucked behind the Jaycees sign, on the rural route
I am a town
I am a town
I am a town
Southbound.

"I Am a Town"
By Mary Chapin Carpenter

TABLE OF CONTENTS

JUST TO BURN IT ALL DOWN

PROLOGUE

On the day this book debuts it will have been six years, six years to the day since the house I loved died.

The memories of that day don't fade as much as they are kept in a different box, a place further back in the attic of the things I remember. But, I don't relive them anymore. I don't smell the smoke and I don't hear the voices or the sirens or my own screaming.

I am spared that, now.

I still see Walker's friends, Cole and Cody, hurdling fire hoses and ignoring demands that they get back, running across the yard to come and stand next to my son as he watched his home burn away. They took off their own shoes on a cold and rainy Carolina November day to provide Walker something to stand on, his bare, size fifteen feet being too big for their Nikes. The three of them stood together, leaning on each other for balance, sharing four shoes. You don't forget sights like that.

Jeff Bolick stopped running the Boxcar Restaurant he owns down by I-40 to man a water hose. He likes to remind me how hard I fought the efforts of the rescue squad as they attempted to give me oxygen and wrap blankets around me. He likes to remind me that even in my darkest hour I can cuss a blue streak without batting an eye. On the night we gathered in his restaurant to hang the football helmet of Greg Issac on the wall of a bar he got kicked out of on more than one occasion, Jeff whispered to me, "I knew you would be all right when I heard you cussin'. I thought, 'she's still in there'."

It's quite a reputation when folks measure your mental health by how many swear words you can fling in a single sentence.

I ought to be ashamed.

I can see the tears running down the cheeks of Gary Sigmon, the crazy Gary Sigmon, not the Claremont Fire Chief, Gary Sigmon. Tough ol' Gary cried for me. His legendary outlaw mentality abandoned him in that hour as he put an arm around me and cried. People left us alone for awhile. Watching knocked everyone's world a little off center, I suppose.

Perhaps it was P.J. Stanley who had it the worst that day. He was the one I assaulted, the one I wanted to lie to me but needed to tell me the truth. With his flannel sleeves gripped in my hands, pulling him to face me, I sobbed for him to tell me the truth, to tell it to me, now, is it too late, is it over, can they save it? All the good on the inside of P.J., whatever it was that always carried him through, it had to take all of it that day because I clearly recall the difficulty he had raising his head, forcing himself to look me in the eye and say, "I believe it's gone."

I should be sorry I made him do that but I'm not sure I would have accepted that truth from anyone else. P.J. wouldn't live to see this book. Before I could finish it we stood around a small wooden box in the cemetery on Main Street and sunk his ashes in the clay. The county newspaper published an editorial I wrote about what his absence would mean to our town. His wife, Brenda, would run into me at the hardware store and thank me for writing it and it would suddenly occur to me that I never returned the coat P.J. had slipped around me, pulling up the hood to keep out the rain that was steady enough to get me wet but no help in saving my house.

The death of my house was made of flames that singed my soul, stripped me of the dead sure belief that all I had to do was work a little harder and be a little smarter to make anything I wanted be true and real.

I sat numb and broken while this town got busy. They thought they were tending to my things. The truth is, they were tending to my fractured heart.

I have an ego as big as The South. I believed that my thirteen-year relationship with the town of Claremont was about the things I did for them: the Author Dinners, the hayrides, the Book Walk, and the Christmas Parties. I thought they had made me a part of their families because of my God-given talent at terrifying people into donating money for scholarships and library funds, that any love they had for me was based on how hard I worked to host Germans from our sister city and how well I decorated the Welcome signs at the edge of town for every season including Race Week, which anyone with good sense knows is a North Carolina State holiday.

I ought to be ashamed.

If the fire taught me that I am not invincible, it is Claremont that taught me I don't have to be. If the fire took away my sense that by being smarter and working harder and making none of the mistakes that less capable people make, I can create a place of complete safety, Claremont taught me I don't need it.

I got people.

I got family.

The most fearless woman in the world saved my life, gave me direction, and became the mother I never had though she was damn quick about pointing out that she was too young for the role. A white-haired woman, most often dressed in pink, set the tables and decorated the church hall and baked a hundred and ninety-two different pound cakes for every event I dreamed up in my self-appointed role as Claremont's Cruise Director. We spent an afternoon sitting on her front porch while she told me the love story of her life with a man we all called Hambone who, by general consensus, cussed more than even me. We elected a Mayor, first by write-in and then, again and again, unopposed and unchallenged in his leadership, who hauled lights and tinsel all the way to Louisiana to see that a hurricane named Katrina hadn't take Christmas with her when she went out to sea. He presided over the bitterly contested Yard of the Month battles until most folks in town either won or gave up, and he opened the doors to a library that gave me the excuse I didn't know I needed and was sure I didn't want to make a phone call and become a part of the town. His wife fixed my sewing mistakes and brought me pass-along-plants and became the best neighbor I've ever had.

Two women, one tall and thin and the other not, tended to me after the fire, shared bleacher space at PTO meetings and basketball games, disagreed with me on every political and social issue that came across the television screen, tried to fix me up with men of their choosing, shook their heads in disappointment when I dumped the nicest guy in the world, and still managed to show me what it means to part of a sisterhood. They shared their young'uns with me and looked after my own like he was kin, and when we discovered that his heart was not as perfect as we had always believed, they prayed as hard as if he were their own and ratted him out when they saw him playing sports against doctor's orders.

A police chief looked the other way if he saw me committing obvious felonies and signed every permit I applied for. He proved to be the very meaning of the phrase "protect and serve" and did so with humor, a framed black and white photograph of Andy and Barney on the wall of his office and daily breakfasts of two thousand calories at Hannah's Bar-B-Q. I openly threatened a City Manager who did not appreciate the fine qualities of the man in charge of our police department. She got gone. The Chief and I remained.

A man I thought I disliked proved to be smart and funny and gave me moonshine and a fine mind to talk to when his wife lost the good sense she had in marrying him and he had to move into the house he used as an office, defying the ordinances of the Claremont Zoning Board for more than ten years. He came to make up for losing Russell, a loss much greater than the burning of my house. His role will always be one of leading man movie star status when he walks across my memory.

I sat on a bedroom floor while a woman in her nineties pulled quilts from dresser drawers and protective pillowcases and spread them across her lap as she told me stories of a Claremont in the time before I knew it. She read a book a week and used the library in traditional form instead of to check email or watch a DVD. She never missed a Tar Heel game or a Sunday morning church service and she never minded when I forgot myself and cussed in front of her.

And, I found a church, of sorts. It was a holy place filled with backsliders and boys who had run more than a trunk load of 'shine in their younger days. Instead of a pew, I took my place at the sacred Back Table, a breach of custom no woman before me had dared. The elders came dressed in overalls and flannel and preached of fast cars and dance hall days and how many fish they caught and deer they put in the freezer. Communion was a cheeseburger all the way or fried bologna or livermush and tea that sent lesser men into a diabetic coma. If I could have loved them more, I would have found a way, and I came to look for any opportunity to show them, to hold them up and into the light. In doing so, I became a writer.

And, if I never do another good or kind thing in my life, which is entirely possible, I can know that because I came to that town for all the wrong reasons and stayed for all the right ones, many song birds found a home and one man found his voice.

The fire took from me the books that sat on every flat surface in my house. No room was without them. They lined shelves and propped up photographs of gone dogs and a grown daughter. They held the secret ingredients in my yellow pepper soup and the best design for a pumpkin patch. They were proof of a time when album covers were art and photographers were artists and John really did love Yoko. They had provided instruction as to refinishing furniture, how to raise quail and cast for trout, and in the case of fourteen copies of the same title, how to know a man by walking around in his skin. They were more company than props, more friend than paper, but what the flames didn't turn to ash, the water hoses drowned beyond saving. It took me weeks to accept, fanning open their pages in a sorry attempt to dry them and make them, and therefore my own self, whole. When I finally gave up and allowed my friends to haul them to the dumpster behind the carwash, only twenty remained, the Holy Fourteen and a collection written by a son of Alabama whose first three pages in a book about his granddaddy pried me loose of a self-imposed exile from people who were waiting to love me and bring me casseroles.

The writers who later came to town, after that September he sat in my kitchen and told me I should be putting words on paper, had come because they wanted to see if Claremont was just some story we'd made up to tell, that Alabama boy and me. They kept on coming, one after another, until it was a common occurrence for a millworker at the Back Table of the Café to be talking about his time in a jungle war with the man who was awarded a Bronze Star for writing about it. Two authors were in Claremont so often they were recognized at the liquor store and asked if they were "stayin' out at Shari's place" though that could have been because they were buying bourbon. I asked a banker for a thousand dollars to get us started putting up bronze plaques commemorating their visits with passages from their books and the dates they came to call, and Tom Winkler and me would drive a city pick up around town and pound them in behind the sidewalks to make the official Claremont Book Walk.

P. J. would lay brick around the one in his yard and make a stained glass light to shine upon it.

The Friends of the Claremont Library would sell tickets in Sunday school class and folks would come to hear the writers read from their books about peach farms and fallen angels, and the Negro baseball league and a voodoo practicing sheriff. Writers would come to town after the fire and fret over me, make me cups of noodle soup and whisper in the hallway about how little of it I was eating. Later, at the new place, they would sit on my back porch, Mason jar in one hand, gesturing for good measure with the other, and talk of book tours and bookstores and how all publishers were sonsabitches and all editors killjoy comma haters and they would each, everyone, not so much encourage me to write so much as threaten bodily harm if I didn't until just to prove them wrong, I sent a story to a magazine.

It sold in an hour, something I have never quite been allowed to live down by a writer who loves the words "told ya so" more than any of the poetry she ever brought to the page.

For reasons that defy good logic, editors kept calling, asking if I had more stories about Claremont and the Café and the ladies of the St. Mark's Quilting Mission. They wanted stories about my daddy and his hunting dogs and the rock collection taking up space on my son's dressers. I wrote tales of moonshiners and broken hearts and escaped poultry and they kept asking for more. When I asked Rita Larkin, a fine editor and funny woman, if I could write about music, she told me to send it her way when it was done and she'd issue the check. Soon a singer/songwriter/storyteller was seen in the Café, once a week or so, pulling his long, white hair back in a ponytail so as not to drag it through the chili and slaw, and a troubadour was getting his picture made in front of my barn for the publicity stills for his next road gig, and brothers, one with a pure voice and the other with a pure heart, were eating soup and cookies at my kitchen table.

A cowboy from Texas sat on my sofa playing a guitar and drinking whiskey and stirring in me a belief, long pronounced dead and buried, while my dogs lay snoring at his feet. Even now, he picks at an un-amplified Stratocaster as I type these words and cry.

I would fall in love with that cowboy and he would sit in a Writer's Shack at the Waterhole Branch of Fish River off Weeks Bay in Alabama and nudge from me, the confession that I had been wrong, again, that there had been music worth listening to written after 1978. Some of it had been penned by the son of a preacher man who spent late night and early morning hours reading to me over the phone as I discovered in him what had been found in me, that we had things to say and sometimes, when everything was right and the moon hung just so and the Southern literary gods favored us, we could write it pretty.

I was born, and remain, a half breed, the daughter of a Tennessee daddy and a Midwestern mother who never took to me. I grew up believing I didn't really belong anywhere.

Claremont was waiting to claim me when I got ready to walk through my own front door. They built a bridge I can cross anytime I feel too far gone, a bridge made of red clay and pines, one that will spark from time to time but never burn, fireproof, constant in its willingness to take me back, welcome me home, even if that home is safest only behind my eyes.

John Hiatt never writes a bad song. This is the one I like best:
"I did not go to college, babe, I did not have the luck.
Stole out of Indiana in the back of a pick-up truck.
No education higher than the streets of my hometown,
I went looking for a fire just to burn it all down."

I found my fire.

I'm not even sorry it happened if this is what I got—this town, these people, these writers and music makers, these stories and the chance to write them, to do my best to honor who they are and what they have taught me, to cross the bridge and show the dignity of those who helped build it, and in doing so, built me, or, at least, put me back together, to sing the praises, as long as it takes and as pretty as I can, of a community of millworkers and farmers and artists until everyone knows the song.

If I don't hit the right notes I ought to be ashamed.

MY PLACE IS
IN THE KITCHEN

Girl children born in the 1960s were not taught how to shoot. Even the most progressive thinking of fathers didn't consider it a rite of passage to stand his daughter up against a board fence so she wouldn't get knocked on her ass, point to a target of straw bales in an open pasture, and tell her to pull the trigger. I walked past the gun cabinet a hundred times a day, begged an uncle or grandfather to hold me up so I could reach the deer head mounted on the wall above it. It was the one corner of the dining room that belonged to men. It held none of the things the women cared about—a great-grandmother's Haviland China or Aunt Maude's cut glass butter dish. No one let me near any of that stuff. I could pet the deer though, could be part of that sacred corner, but only with the help of a man.

My father was an excellent shot, and everyone in the county knew it to be true. I don't remember anyone having to tell me how straight his aim was. I just always knew. There were trophies in a case he built for himself, trophies of his countless wins at trap-shooting events. He let me play with those sometimes, rearrange them, read the inscriptions when I was older. Freezers stayed packed full of turkeys and hams, his winnings from shooting. Neighbors, too, shared in the spoils. When a pig got out of a fence and was hit by a car, maimed but not killed, those same neighbors came to get my dad to put it out of its misery. It was his job to do the killing of the steers on butchering day. My Papaw bought him a gun, special for the task. My daddy could shoot.

I remember standing at his side many times during his never-ending battle with groundhogs. He explained to me that the holes to their tunnels were a danger to the horses and a danger to me if I was riding. I'm pretty sure he just plain hated them, their holes as good an excuse as any to shoot them dead. He would rest against that board fence and whisper, "Hold your ears, Sissy, I'm fixin' to nail him to the cross."

Shootin' things was men's work. I never thought to ask why.

Truth is, I didn't want so much to kill anything as be a part of it all, the ritual of cleaning the guns, the packing for the hunting trips, the loading of the shotgun shells and that Holy Grail, the tackle box. My dad had a tackle box bigger than anyone who fished with him, and in my mind, and in reality, you could have survived Armageddon using what was in that box. Four tiers of compartments splayed out on each side of the thing when opened, and because my dad and his dad, and me for that matter, carry a tradition of being resourceful types, that tackle box contained genius.

Dad discovered—I don't know how but suspect it originated in dares due to alcohol consumption—that a container of Old Spice stick deodorant was not only airtight and watertight, but that the damn thing would float. Once it had served the purpose of keeping him from stinking, it was cleaned out and fashioned into a holder for matches. "You never, ever, want your matches to get wet," he would say to me as he filled it and put it in the exact right compartment.

My people tend to lean toward the obsessive.

An empty pill bottle held cotton balls soaked in petroleum jelly so those desert-dry matches could be put to use. Knives were so sharp I was not allowed to hold them, even in their sheaths. Dad put his name on everything using one of those label-makers, the kind you had to dial to get the right letter and then squeeze with both hands to make an impression on black tape. I loved to see him get out the tackle box and prepare for a trip. I would sit on the floor watching, listening to him talk about this lure and that reel. I cannot remember one valuable piece of information, nothing that would be of any use in catching a fish or shooting a deer. I just loved hearing him talk.

Before he left, I would say, "If you find an orphan deer, will you bring it home for me?" He would promise to do exactly that, and then they would be gone, all of them, and I would be stuck with a family full of women.

They talked about people, the women in my family. They didn't speak of how straight their rows of corn were or how clean they kept their tool sheds. They never commented on the weather, never held a hand over their eyes for shade and said, "I believe that one is a red-tail." They didn't sit on the porch in the swing, cigarette glowing in the coming darkness, listen to the quail in the orchard and ask, "Can you hear them? Listen, now. Can you hear him say, "Bob WHITE, Bob WHITE?"

No, their entertainment was a full-throttle thrashing of everyone living that they could think to name, and when they ran out of breathing folks they moved on to the transgressions of the deceased. The women in my family never forget anything.

In a week, sometimes two, the men would be coming home, and I would stand at the window, staring down the gravel road until my grandmother would say to sit down, I was worryin' her to death. Any sign of a vehicle meant it was more than likely the men. Heavy traffic was not an issue on our road. Soon, but not soon enough, there they'd be, unloading the take, carrying in the coolers.

That's when it got good.

If you were a quiet girl child, and I learned to be just that for this purpose, you could sit on the top steps of the basement and listen to the talk. They knew I was there. They must have. I don't recall much swearing. (It was my great aunt Marvel, a fine, fine old woman, who taught me to cuss like a sailor. She chain-smoked, had a voice to prove it and mailed me books wrapped in brown paper.) There was excitement in these first hours home. I had to be patient, wait for them to settle down and get to the real story-telling. It was always, every time, worth the wait.

They did not teach me to shoot. Instead, I learned to measure flour. Biscuits, that's the first thing a girl on the farm learns to make. After my debut batch, my Daddy said he believed those were the best biscuits he "ever eat," and not being a stupid child, I kept baking.

As long as food was brought to the table they would stay there and talk. If you brought glasses of tea to the tool shed, they would take a minute to drink and talk. I could listen because I had to wait for them to finish so as not to leave my grandmother's glasses on the work bench. Only I forgot. Often. So when I was threatened with violence if I took any more of her precious Tupperware tumblers to the barn, I learned to open the refrigerator in the basement, the one that held only small bottles of Coca-Cola, stand on a chair to use the bottle opener bolted to a wooden block on the concrete wall, and tote as many cokes as there were men fixing something somewhere.

Grandfathers died, uncles divorced their way out of the family, and a stroke took from my father his gift for hitting anything at which he pointed a gun. Men don't come home from the hunt anymore. I don't hear their footsteps on my porch, stomping off the mud, putting down the coolers. That is gone and I miss it.

My father didn't write any books of his adventures. He was too busy working 18-hour shifts in the factory, and coming home to help his father and his father-in-law work their farms, my maternal grandfather's own children being too sorry to be much help at anything, the root of my hatred for laziness. There are no written pages with the stories my father told, the stories he lived.

Instead, his guns serve as his books and I have them. I cannot shoot them, but I have them, and they tell me the story of the log that was sticking out of the water in a lake in Canada, the log my daddy thought might lurk large enough beneath the surface to damage a boat and so fired up the motor to steer around it. As he did so, he watched the log become a bull moose and rise from the waters that kept the flies off his back. I know that story real good. I know them all. The women in my family never forget anything.

Now, on the back half of my 40s, I am dependent on the writings of Guy de la Valdene and Jimbo Meador. I am stuck waiting, waiting for the next book Charles Gaines will write, the next magazine article published, the next story John Currence will tell of the camaraderie and laughter, of the tradition and the table. I can only wait.

That girl child still stands at the window and looks down a gravel road. But now it is the UPS man who kicks up dust as he brings to her the stories of the hunt, books wrapped in brown paper.

MY BROTHER'S KEEPER

The Police Chief likes to tell the story of how he set about running off a drunk in town, a carpetbagger, by making the competition known to the *Official* Town Drunk who knew, and made clear, that Claremont was, and is, only big enough for one of them.

We got rules.

Our current town drunk is Raymond. I don't know his last name and it doesn't much matter as most people around here go by one name anyway, most likely a nickname of which no one can remember the origin. In the winter, Raymond lets his white hair grow long. It calls to mind Albert Einstein's choice in hairstyles. Raymond wears an army jacket, a parka, and walks down the street pointing to all kinds of landscaping and stop signs and talking to himself. He might be talking to the bushes or the flowers in the churchyard, it's hard to tell. He walks with purpose, pointing first with his right hand and then with his left and talks in the general direction of the ground he is carefully watching. If you call to him and wave from your truck window, he will stop pointing and wave and he will say "hey" when spoken to, though it barely disrupts the conversation he is having with people we cannot see.

Raymond lives in a storage unit down by the highway. This is his choice. He has a job and makes good money but he likes things the way they are. Jerry, at The Café, is fond of saying that Raymond lives in "a gated community" and everybody always laughs like he just said it for the first time. On nights when it is cold, too cold, the police chief calls the owners of the local Super 8, the only motel for several Interstate exits, and has one of the boys on patrol go and fetch Raymond. He stays warm on those nights. I don't know how cold it has to get. The Chief must have a low temperature in mind or maybe he doesn't. Maybe he goes by his bones. The Chief has awful good bones for things like that.

Before Raymond, our town drunk was Archie, but we lost him a few months ago. There was a bit of overlap in the role of Town Drunk but Archie didn't mind as he was sober for the last several weeks of his life. There is nobody in town who doesn't have a story of going to pick up Archie from somewhere and toting him home to his upstairs apartment in the building his momma left to him. We didn't mind making sure he got home in one piece. He never went far, not since coming home in '71, I think, little more than a boy, from a jungle war he had no part in choosing, a war that changed him. Miss Janie said he got out of the car on the corner of Depot and Main, dropped to his knees on the concrete and kissed the sidewalk, swearing he would never again leave Claremont.

He wasn't much for sober after that.

Archie would get locked up every now and then but somebody, one of the good people that live in this town, would gather bail money and get him out. He spent a lot of time in the VA hospital. He spent a lot of time in the Kangaroo convenience store on that same corner he kissed. He spent a lot of time at the Back Table of The Café. It was his absence from these, his regular spots, that sent Glenn Overcash and Willie Hewitt to the police station. They told those who protect and serve that they were kicking in Archie's door, with or without police assistance, and so they were the ones to find him.

He'd been sober two months. That was too long, I suppose.

Raymond works the night shift and comes in The Café to sleep as soon as they open the doors around five or so. We let him sleep, his head on the table, his arms wrapped around his ears to keep out the noise and the light. When he wakes up he orders eggs and grits, eats them, and takes to walking the streets of Claremont, North Carolina talking to the unseen and drinking beer behind Glenn's shop. Glenn told him he could drink there all he wanted but he had to start picking up the cans and throwing them away.

We got rules.

Before Archie, the town drunk was Goober Green. The Hokes who own The Café took care of him, built him a little ten by ten house out back when people calling themselves caretaking Christians wouldn't allow a drunk to live in the same house with his own sick momma. It was the only way, they said. They would take proper care of Miss Pearl, her spine, bent and twisted, so she could die in her own pretty house with the wraparound porch and fishscale shingles and they would get the deed when she went on to Glory, but her son could not live there. He was on a first name basis with the devil, they believed. I reckon they could easily see that from their high and mighty position. They didn't have to wait long to claim ownership. Maybe Miss Pearl knew that striking the deal would hasten her death, a woman known to sit just outside the back screen door, dipping snuff and spitting at a flat rock a good ten feet from the porch boards under her rocker. I'm told she had dead aim. Goober was tended to and it was a lot more convenient. With the little shack right there in the parking lot, he could stumble from the Pool Room to the bed they set up for him. Goober Green died at the VA and is buried next to his mother in the cemetery on Main Street. I know because I went looking for him and found him right where Miss Jo Marilyn told me he would be.

The pretty house on the corner with the wraparound porch and the fishscale shingles would be first sold to one and then another and finally to a couple from Minnesota who sold it to me. It was the excuse people used to talk to me. They would tell me of the time the driver of a something, something car misjudged the corner and ran up on the porch, knocking Goober out of his bed, a fright that had him to tell the county newspaper that it scared him so bad his false teeth dropped right out of his mouth. They would tell me how Miss Pearl had the unexplained ability to take the fire out of burns, and that she predicted that God would strike a man blind who was looking at things he ought not, but how with all of her powers she could not make her son stop drinking, nor take the consumption from the lungs of her daughter, who lay in the front bedroom with smooth rocks from the Catawba River warmed in the cookstove on her heaving chest—for comfort and relief from the disease that killed her. They told me that Miss Pearl sure would like it that I lived in that house, that she would want someone there who loved the wide plank wood floors and fancy corbels in the peaks of the high pitch of the roof. They told me she would have liked me when I finally let them talk to me, when I finally let them in.

We take care of folks in this town. We give them rides and bail them out and make sure they have shelter. If we could we would make the sounds of gunfire and the visions of their friends dying go away, but some things are beyond even the good people of Claremont—not much, mind you, but some things. And, if someone moves into town and keeps to herself, keeps her window shades drawn and her truck parked in back and appears as though she doesn't want company, we don't give up trying. Gary Sigmon would say there ain't no call to.

It wasn't Sunday school or police training that taught Claremont to be their Brother's Keepers. Most folks are born knowing what is right. Some have to come to a small town in rural North Carolina and be reminded that there are people who come with good bones.

Claremont is a town full of good bones.

MESS WITH ME, YOU MESS WITH THE WHOLE TRAILER PARK

I am in the barn by 6:30 on most mornings. I am back in the house by 7:15, and if it's Saturday, the channel is set to 53, HGTV, by 7:30.

It runs all day.

Walker's posse used to make disparaging comments about my refusal to change the channel even if I never watch a complete show. They asked me why it has to be on HGTV if I am doing my own painting or gardening or recovering project. They said it was dumb. I said I had four words for them:

E—S—P—N.

The pot ceased to level any more insults at the kettle.

I pore over magazines and tape paint swatches to the drywall to see how the color changes as the sun moves across the sky and even though I told Walker there would be no major renovations in this house, that it didn't need any, there he was, knocking down a wall two weeks ago, at my request, to make a big kitchen even bigger.

I think of it as a hobby, an interest—maybe an obsessive interest—but it is not how I measure worth, mine or anyone else's. I know better.

Of the regulars at my supper table, the boys who drop their gym bags at the back door and know they are welcomed, loved, and that their future birthdays might be cut short if they piss me off, only the Isenhour twins and Cole McGraw live in houses with foundations. There are wheels under the rest of them.

The first time we took Joe Litton home from a ball game and turned down a dirt road I didn't know existed, through pines that blocked out the stars in the night sky, I told Joe how nice it must be to live back that far. He said it sure was. We pulled up to the trailer where Joe lives with his momma on his granddaddy's land and saw the goats in the fence behind his home. I asked if they were fainting goats and Joe said they were but, "They don't faint no more. We opened the back door and yelled at them too many times, just to see 'em faint, and they got used to it and quit faintin'."

Joe can throw a football so pretty it makes grown men cry. He won the Pirate Award when they were eighth graders for his achievement as a student athlete. He is the one I trust with this farm and my critters when I go out of town, and when I come home everything is in apple pie order. The dog that never leaves my side runs to the door when she sees Joe come through. While the rest of the gang are procrastinating on their assignments, Joe is sitting at a computer, writing papers for me to later check and make suggestions, though he barely needs any. He wants to get his teaching degree so he can be a coach and the first person in his family to graduate from college.

I told his coach and the A.D. that I would do illegal and immoral things to make certain it all happens for that boy. The A.D. laughed. The coach did not. I think I scared him a little.

Donovan lives with his rock steady daddy and his take-no-prisoners momma in a double wide. They drive much better vehicles than I have, go out to dinner and movies whenever they choose, and will be debt free before they are fifty-two years old. I will be paying for my house when I am a hundred and twenty-seven. Jeff and Evelyn Rinehardt are deciding what they want to do when Donovan moves out; sell their place and travel, move closer to Greensboro and their smart and beautiful daughter, or stay put and owe nothing to nobody.

If you locked the most hardened racists in a room with Donovan and

Walker for a day, they would emerge fighting to be the new president of the Rainbow Coalition. To watch them, to listen to the two of them, is to know no boundary of color or culture. Walker and Donovan are brothers. They are different and they are exactly the same and I would steal Donovan and claim him as my own but his momma would hunt me down and hurt me.

At a church service for a teammate's mother who had cancer, Walker and Donovan sat beside one another. Evelyn and I sat behind them. We were in the Baptist church in Catawba and other than members of the team, the coach and his family, and Stephanie LaFone, Walker and I were only the white faces in the tiny, overcrowded room. The music was so good it might could get me to go to church and I honestly feared that Walker would answer the altar call.

When the gospel choir fired up, Donovan leaned over to Walker and whispered something. Walker pushed him away, looked insulted and said something Evelyn and I could not hear. She leaned forward and asked Donovan what was going on.

"I told Walker he could clap along with the music or not clap along, but he better stay with the beat and not embarrass me. Walker said he knew when to clap cause he's not that white."

Their mommas laughed like fools through the next song.

Jeremy's house is manufactured, though it doesn't much look like it. Phillip and his family used to live in a double wide, the prettiest place you've ever seen, but they sold it a few years ago and moved into new construction near Conover. Those are some good and gifted boys. Say something insulting to Jeremy Null, and he might hurl a fastball at your head. Say something insulting to Phillip and he will pray for you.

Or, quote a Monty Python movie—either way, you'll feel like an idiot.

I recently reconnected with a friend from high school. I think he was my boyfriend for twelve minutes in the sixth grade. I think I wore his dog tag around my neck.

He owns several trailer parks, buys them, fixes them to perfection, and sees that they are lovely communities for the people who live there. Seems he works all day every day and hopes to take his pretty wife and travel in a couple of years, go to beaches and mountains, and fly his Ultra-light and drive his sexy Corvette. He is well informed, a great dad, and a good thinker, and I am just about as proud of him and happy for him as I have been of anyone in a long time. I think he is the straw that stirs the liquor, by God, and elevates the entire class of '79 just by getting to claim him.

A woman came to my house for a party not too far back. She got dead drunk and spent the night draped over someone else's husband whose wife was five feet away. She referred to herself as a debutante. She lives at the country club in a half-million-dollar spread with white furniture and tasteful decor.

One of my exes lives in 8,000 square feet with an indoor pool and spent tens of thousands flipping the back to the front so he wouldn't have to see the lesser houses that border his neighborhood when he drives his Maserati into the gated driveway. He recently had his teeth "done" and called in sick and worked from home for a week after a dye job went horribly wrong. My son remembers him making fun of a little boy with brittle bone disease, calling him "that ugly little unathletic boy," and screaming at his new wife when she misread a map and they missed a turn on a family vacation.

You tell me who's trash.

I'm going to paint the new part of the kitchen today. I love the shade of red I chose. It's perfect. It matches the barn *and* the wallpaper in the old part of the kitchen; it will tie together the outdoors with the in and will look *fabulous* when they do a magazine photo shoot later on this month.

And the best part, the part I'm most proud of, is that I know it is only a can of paint and not an indication of character...or value.

KATE

We said goodbye to Kate this morning. She was ready.

I was not.

Big Pond's Cannonball Kate came to us when my dear friend, Ann Viklund, thought she would help me get over the grief for my own Paja, then a year gone. Kate had earned her master hunter title, been a good mother to two big litters of puppies—eight in one, 13 in the other—and brought back vests full of ducks for Ann's husband, Max, Kate's trainer and friend. It was time for her to find a sofa cushion on which to sleep and shed, and time for me to love another good old working dog.

But Kate, too much woman to be anybody's second pick, chose my son. She had a boy, and Walker, after 13 years of living in a house full of dogs, had one that liked him best, best of all.

If Walker threw the retrieving dummy a hundred times a day, Kate fetched it up every time, limping as fast as an arthritic shoulder would carry her, wagging her tail when he took it from her, begging him to throw it again. He would nag at me until I abandoned whatever I was doing to come and hold Kate, turning her away so she couldn't see as

Walker would hide the dummy in the bushes or the hedges or one of the flower beds I had recently gardened to perfection. Walker had himself a retriever. Kate, she had her very own boy.

She would stand in front of him as he watched television in the late evenings, telling him it was time for bed, and to my amazement Walker would give in, "OK, old girl. Guess you're tired." When her shoulder would no longer allow her the leap onto his bed, Walker would pick her up, placing her head on a pillow, pull the covers over the two of them and there she would stay until morning. There's many a night I don't think she moved.

As recently as last weekend she would choose his room for sleep, even when it was full of the friends he has had since kindergarten. I would open the door in the mornings to find Kate in a tangle of arms and legs in sleeping bags, boxer shorts, and Braves T-shirts, once with her paw right square on Cole McGraw's forehead, her back against Walker's, sharing his pillow, all of them open-mouth snorin'.

Cole's brother, Hayden, enough younger to wear on the tolerance of boys five years his senior, turned to Kate when they turned on him. Leaving on his own accord or being banished from their talk of girls and Carolina basketball, Hayden would find her on the couch, slide under Kate's heavy, sleeping head and stroke her neck, leaning over her to whisper the secrets boys tell only to dogs, secrets I could not hear from my place in the kitchen. Kate would eventually sit up next to Hayden, putting her head against his, making it hard to tell the stopping and starting of her coat and his blonde head. Hayden would call to me, wanting a witness, "She likes me," and I would say she sure does. Kate knew when to be a momma.

Hayden will grow to be a dog man. You can just tell. I'm not quite sure where it comes from, the love of dogs, the pull to stand in the cold, in rain and worse just to watch them work. Maybe it is born in you. Maybe it is handed down through stories. Either way, my own adoration for a dog that knows an honest day's work comes from my daddy and the tales of dogs I only know through legend, from begging him to "Tell it, again" when he insisted I already knew the story of the best pointer he ever saw.

I know from listening that hunters fret when hunting over a dog unfamiliar to them. My father was no different and worried about the doctor who came to hunt the farm ground my family worked to put food on the table and in the silos for winter. Dad can still tell it like he saw it an hour ago, the pointer so sure he was moving in the right direction that he climbed the farm fence, paid no mind to the barbwire stretched across the top, and froze there, balanced in a point, trying with all he had to tell the men that the birds they hunted were there on the other side.

Unable to hold his balance, the dog fell to the ground and to the sky rose a covey of 25 birds. "We was so amazed at that dog and what we was seeing, not one of us could get a gun up." The dog hung his head in shame at having flushed the covey, failing in the impossible feat of holding point on a stretch of barbwire. They gave him a pat, all the forgiveness he needed, and they hunted over him, finding singles for the rest of the day. That was 50 years ago, but when my daddy tells the story I can smell the cold and see the wire sway with the weight of a dog doing his best on a hunt that took place before I was born.

When my father was a teenager, a barber gave him a pup out of his female known to be the best coon dog in the county. She'd been bred to Jack, a black and tan "registered" dog that won every field trial he entered and served as the standard to which all treeing dogs were measured. My daddy was in high cotton, a teenager with a pup out of Jack, and in six months had him running a trail and treeing alone in the woods that bordered the cornfields of my grandfather's farm—his only fault being a reluctance to leave the glow of the light for the first hour. He has lived on in my mind, dead now more than 60 years, because dog men love to tell of the good ones as much as they love to watch them work.

There was Old Jerry, the farm dog, a cur, so loyal to my grandfather he walked every round behind the tractor my Pa drove to plow the fields. "He wouldn't follow me, no," my father always says. "He only trailed Daddy." Jerry tolerated a goat harness and would pull a wagon or a snow sled hauling children to destinations unknown. Had he spent his days on the porch or under a shade tree he would be remembered as a lazy dog, and lazy don't count for much in my family. Instead, he was a working dog, the farm dog, and earned his place in our history by guarding ground that kept us fed, and running off intruders who looked like they wasn't to be trusted.

I have been handed the right to call these dogs my own because I am the one who remembers them, the one who knows their stories, and I reckon, whether it is biology or brainwashing, I am the one who carried the love of working dogs into the next generation, who filled her house with dogs that do something, dogs that earn their keep, even if, like Kate, their working days were over before they came to sleep on my couch and love my boy.

I couldn't put this good girl in the ground, not when she so loved water and wings. They will send her up the smokestack this afternoon and what they give back to me, the dust of her, belongs to two people.

A handful of Kate I will put in the garden of black-eyed Susans outside Walker's window, the one closest to his bed. The rest of her will ride with me to Grandfather Mountain where the wind is always blowin', blowin' hard.

I'll let her go, let the wind take her back to southern Illinois, back to Max Viklund in time for hunting season. Kate will fly there with the ducks, the ones who always before got away.

THE TROUBLE
WITH AMERICA

I tend to like to do things myself. It irritates me to find that I am without the skill or physical strength to do what needs doing, another example of my control issues.

I don't care.

Needing the stall built quickly and well, I hired help. The goal had been a horse home no 'Feed Me *NOW*' fit could bring down. A good man who knows how to swing a hammer was what I needed. What I got was an expert. On *everything*.

I casually mentioned the price of lumber on his first day of measuring and got twenty minutes of monologue on The Trouble with America. I didn't know that the price of lumber was, in fact, the ruination of this country, but apparently I have not been paying attention. I also failed to recognize that teenagers who throw toilet paper in the trees of their friends' houses are The Trouble with America, the hiring practices of Bell South are The Trouble with America, and the change in cheeseburgers at The Café since Miss Janie retired are, indeed, The Trouble with America.

I also learned that I do nothing right. Not a damn thing. I don't paint my fence correctly or mow my pasture to suit nor do I read good books. He bragged to me one day that he had over 5,000 titles, not books, mind you, but *titles* of paperback science fiction and had read them all.

If nobody gets so drunk they run over their own mailbox or shoots, skins, and fries something, chances are, I ain't read it. I told him this at The Café and a man sitting at another table laughed out loud.

For the first couple of days, it was tolerable. That passed. I am nothing if not my father's child. You get up and work. Critters need feeding, something needs cleaning, the world needs saving. Get up and get to it. My contractor showed up around noon on good days and more often between two and five. Said he had (1) another job, (2) a broke down van, (3) called Bingo down at the lodge the night before and was wore out. But he made up for his lack of dependability by knowing absolutely everything about absolutely everything.

For example:

Quail nest on top of one another in a big ol' pile and one of the males walks circles around them as a "sentry." (They don't.) A group of white kids is fine, but a group of black kids always gets into trouble. (They don't.) If you don't pay your property taxes, the government will come in and seize your stuff, sell it, and keep the money. (They do, but that is the Trouble with America.)

The day he told me to check for the leak in the water pipe that ran to the barn by listening for a clicking sound I almost told him that was the sound of the facial tic I was developing by keeping company with him. When I broke a glass Mason jar on the concrete of my son's basketball court and cleaned it up with a broom, dustpan, and shop vac, he told me I would need a leaf blower to properly get the job done. When I answered his question as to why I had a Mason jar in the barn by telling him it was so I could measure a full quart of each type of food for my horse, I discovered that I had hired Roy Damn Rogers.

He told me I didn't need to be so exact, that horses could tolerate eating anything. (They can't.) He said that his version of the grate for the window opening was good enough because horses don't try to push things. (They do, and it wasn't.) That was our Come to Jesus.

I eventually paid him to just go away but not before I was treated to the single most impressive piece of stupidity known to mankind.

Yesterday, during lunch at the Back Table of The Café, the subject turned to politics. I usually do my best to goad one or two of them into a throwdown, an absolute verbal slugfest that always ends with Melvin Little yelling, "You wouldn't think that if you were old enough to remember Hoover."

That one kills me every time.

Anyway, this time, I wanted to avoid it because I had vowed to beat him into a coma if he, one more time, told me what The Trouble with America was, and with what I was paying him, I was short on bail money. One blamed it on Bush and the next one blamed it on Obama and I hummed a little song to myself, Miranda Lambert's "It's Time to Get a Gun," while he, The Expert, put in his two cents. When he was winding down, I turned to Jim Sigmon, eighty years old, and said, "They can't blame you for any of it, can they Mr. Jim? You voted for Hillary, didn't you?" and he said, "I sure did, yes, ma'am."

The contractor said, "Well, now, that was a wasted vote. If she can't even keep her husband satisfied at home, if you know what I mean, how is she supposed to take care of the rest of us?"

I checked to see if my ears were bleeding. A sly smile crept across Jim Sigmon's face as he sat back, crossed his arms, and said, "You're in for it now."

Turns out I didn't need bail money. Every woman who has ever been cheated on, Democrats and Republicans, Independents and Libertarians, Jews and Gentiles, pooled their money and I was free as a bird. It was a sight to see, all of them joined together down at the magistrate's office, a real thing of homespun Americana beauty. The judge was a right-wing, gun-totin' redneck who hated Leftie Communists more than she loved lowering taxes but when she heard that he blamed the Bill's wife for his eight-year frat party in the Oval Office, she dismissed the case and said she was real sorry for the bother. I emerged from the courthouse to a throng of women, all ages, all beliefs, joined together in a heartwarming lynch mob ready to finish what I started … at least, that was the scene that played out in my mind as he drove out the lane for the last time, puttered on down the road in his foreign-made car, allowed to keep breathing and sadly keep talking and talking and talking.

But, that is The Trouble with America.

STILL WALKER

What are little boys made of? Spiders and frogs and lightning bugs, that's what little boys, and the grownups they become, are made of.

So I gave him a job.

The boards I saved from the scrap heap, the wood that once formed a fence for Miss Jean that I carried across the street, two at a time, are going to become the inside walls of the new guest barn. I asked Walker to carry them behind our fence and stack them neatly on a wooden table to ready them for the chop saw.

Three minutes. It took him three minutes to find something and come fetch me.

He used to hit the door flyin'. "Momma! Momma, come and see, and hurry. I found a (fill in the blank)."

I was summoned for a garden spider when he was almost four. He named her Charlotte and had a bagel every morning as he watched her make her kill. We looked up everything we could find about the black-and-yellow Argiope, and when she laid an egg sack and became half her size, I lied to the boy and did not tell him that she was dead and the daddy had taken her place. I lied to him again the next year when he found another one and believed it was Charlotte come back, because he had cared for her so gently by building a shelter around her web when the winds of a faraway hurricane threatened those babies he waited on.

I lied to him four more times, four more falls until he looked it up in the *National Audubon Society Field Guide to North American Insects and Spiders* and learned the truth. He wasn't mad at me. He was mad at the book.

My presence has been commanded for box turtles and snakeskins and walking sticks. I've been called to save half-dead baby birds and witness the increase in the size of a woodpecker hole in the twenty minutes since the last time he insisted I "come quick," and was once subjected to the sight of my boy tenderly cradling a nest of baby moles, despite my world-famous, mind-numbing, bone-crushing fear of rodents, because he reasoned "moles aren't mice," as I scrubbed his little hands with Brillo pads and Clorox.

His room has always held the poorly kept secrets of boyhood: rocks, each with more magic than the last; shells, of turtles and of the beach; lightning bugs in Mason jars; a praying mantis in a shoebox; and all the reference books he needed to irritate the hell out of lesser-informed guests with his vast knowledge of all creatures great and small.

Today, at soon-to-be-16, he has come in the house seven times during what should have been a thirty-minute task. He found the perfect shell of a cicada and thought I should see it in the state in which he found it in case it tore when he tried to pick it up. It didn't. It now sits on a stack of books, the *Shiloh* trilogy, behind the glass door of a cabinet that first belonged in a woman's kitchen in 1931. I have some doubts about her willingness to immortalize a cicada where her fine china used to be, but who I am to say?

A katydid, a dead hornet "with all the fuzz still attached," an impressive worm hole in the wood, an impressive worm, a click beetle and what he is sure is the hole of a blacksnake have all propelled him from his assigned task and through the front door yelling, "Hey Mom, don't murder me, but you gotta see this."

I lie to him still. I pretend he is driving me nuts, that I don't want to be taken from my work at this computer and called to witness the latest in his fascinations. I roll my eyes and he laughs a little and I walk behind him so that he doesn't see his momma tearing up as she remembers how little and blond and happy he was from the moment he was born. I say, "Yes, Walker, it is truly a remarkable (fill in the blank), and now that I have been treated to this wonder of nature, can I return, you know, to paying the bills?"

I wonder how long it will be until I am not his first call, by cell phone or ear-piercing holler. I recall days when his language was his own and he came running into the kitchen, insisting that cooking could wait, that I needed to watch a primate program on the Discovery Channel. "It's a whole hour, Momma, a whole hour just on pin-chan-gees." I had to look to his big sister for translation. He was so proud of his knowledge of White House history when, at four, he told us that the 16th President of the United States was "Hammerhead Lincoln," that I threatened the lives of his teachers if he learned otherwise. For the remainder of Walker's pre-school year, the teachers referred to Honest Abe as "Hammerhead" and I am not sorry for it.

That sweet child is in there, that boy who slept with stuffed animals he named for the greatness of Carolina: Mitchell the bear, Chimney Rock the mountain lion, River C. the owl, and the beaver named Grandfather. His television is permanently tuned into *Sports Center*, and he shoots hoops more than he fishes, but he is there.

I saw him today.

ABOUT PEACE

For a smart girl I can be a real dumbass.

Boonie Miller has eaten at least one meal a day, six days a week, every one of his fifty some years at the Claremont Café. If you're looking for proof that man can survive on a diet of lard and starch, Boonie Miller is it. I like Boonie, always have. Boonie does doughnuts with his truck in the city hall parking lot when it snows real heavy and is good to explain protocol to first timers in The Café when they sit down and actually think someone is going to come to their table to wait on them. He has been married to Lisa for twenty or more years.

Six years ago her daddy went missing.

He was a strange old character, did things his own way and had the cash to pay for it. He owned quite a bit of land east of town and spent his days at The Café and his nights in the Pool Room or down at Boxcar Grill near the highway, not all that different from many others here in Claremont. Not so much for the church-goers but for the backsliders, Wayne Connor's life was fairly typical.

His dog was home and half starved. His truck was parked in his driveway, his answering machine had seventeen calls, and his keys and wallet must have been with him when he got gone for they were never found. They figured it had been six days since anybody could recall seeing him when Boonie finally took the key from Lisa's trembling hand and went in to see if his wife's daddy had a heart attack or drank himself to death.

It was like he vanished.

They did all the things heartsick people do. They called, they cried, they walked the piney woods of Catawba County calling his name, but nothing, no where, has ever been found. There are as many theories as there are citizens in Claremont, but it has stumped law enforcement at city, county, state, and federal levels. Twice a week, Lisa calls the detective on the case to see if there is any news. If he is out to lunch, he returns the call. He must be a good soul, that man, because he does call her back.

I had been reading Joe Galloway's first book, *We Were Soldiers...Once and Young*. Joe is a good friend of mine. The only civilian awarded the Bronze Star, Joe is a badass who likes whiskey and smart women and puts out his cigarette with the toe of his cowboy boot, but will weep openly over the brothers he made in a battle that would be known only to those who fought it had Joe passed on writing the book or giving the okay to the movie. He is all of that and a damn fine writer but it was a slow read for me. Despite having the vocabulary of a truck driver and a take-no-prisoners reputation, I am a fake, a phony.

I am a poser.

My heart is a tender, soft place capable of breaking into so many pieces you'd need a good tracking dog to find them all. Sometimes, most times, when reading Joe's book it was hard to turn the page for fear of what was coming.

I wanted it to stop, the gunfire, long enough for me to catch my breath. I wanted Joe to stop writing about the bullets, the way they tore through boys who must have looked like my own, and I would try and comfort myself by looking for clues in the tense of Joe's style whether a soldier lived, that he lives still, a way of coping I suppose with a story that needed telling.

It was pretty self absorbed, to sit in my comfortable living room by a warm fire and think I had any right to wish it would stop, to hope that Joe Galloway would give me just a small break in the carnage and the death and the grief, time to find a moment of peace in a book I could close and put down anytime I wanted and skip on over to the kitchen for a glass of sweet tea. It was shameful, but not the worst of my self indulgence.

Every time I listened to Joe speak about those men going under fire to retrieve the dead I believed that, were I in charge, I would have had better sense. It defied logic for me, why the good Hal Moore, then a colonel, now a lieutenant general, would risk more lives to gather up the corpses of those already lost. Dead is dead. Bringing them home in a box would not give their wives more babies to rock or fill another seat at their momma's Thanksgiving table. Seemed a waste to me, seemed wrong no matter how much respect I had for what they went through in those days and nights, no matter how many pages I forced myself to turn to understand what it was like ... I could not bring myself to think that sending the living after the dead had been the right choice.

Boonie and Lisa Miller sat down with me at the Claremont Café one day while I was reading the book. Boonie commented on the high worth of his fried bologna by calling our attention to the amount of grease that had soaked through the paper. "That's how you know it's gonna be gooooood."

I reckoned so.

Lisa asked me to explain what it is I do, how is it that I justify my existence in the literary world. She has met a truckload of writers who have come to town to rock or write on my porch. She once had her picture made and put in the local paper with Karen Spears Zacharias, so on this day, after she had given up on trying to find any good reason for me to be earning a paycheck, she asked about Karen, trying to remember their conversation.

"She lost her daddy, too, right?"

"Yes," I said. "He was killed in Vietnam."

"Did she get him back?"

Even now, the sound of her voice rings in my head and hits me square in the center of my fragile heart. I hadn't been looking at her when she asked it. I'd been searching for the best way to pick up a sandwich too full to stay inside the confines of a bun. I don't know how I knew but I did, I did know what her face would look like when I raised my eyes to hers.

I'll bet that I will see Lisa Miller a million times before one of us ain't here no more. I'll run into her at the fish camp or the bluegrass show in the parking lot. I will sit with her and Boonie while we take years off our lives by eating at The Café, but I will forever think of her in that moment.

Her eyes were pleading and her stare was one of needing me to say that, yes, a daughter could get her daddy back even if it was in a box, even if he was in pieces. He might could come home.

Sometimes, you get them back.

Afraid to speak, I nodded. Tears came anyway so I choked out, "Yes, Lisa, she sure did. She got him back."

"I'm glad," she told me. "I'm glad he came home."

I'm not going to whine anymore about wanting the bullets to stop in Joe's books or movies. I will turn every page he writes until the story is told and I will never again believe that my way would have been smarter, that it would have been a better choice to leave a man behind, a man who isn't breathing.

For those who were called and answered out of a sense of duty or for fear they couldn't learn to speak Canadian, believing they were coming home through hell and high water was all they had. For the man who seemed to just disappear from the slap middle of town, it's all that's left. Lisa Miller, decades and oceans away from the LZ in a book by Joe Galloway, taught me that it isn't about logic and it isn't about war.

It is about peace.

TRASH CAN FAIRIES
AND PECAN PIES

I have a lot more land now.

I have acres of pasture and woods and a house with so many bed-rooms I forget what's in them if I skip the weekly dusting. I have a family room and a dining room and a living room which my friend, Edie, calls my library, four toilets and ten sinks to clean, and a jetted bathtub deep enough to drown in. When Edie brings me magazines with decorating ideas, we sit in my big country kitchen and look out so many windows that when I hang red, white, and blue bunting for the Fourth of July it looks like a patriot threw up on my house. I have a deck and a porch and a barn and a tree house for Matilda.

But I used to have a neighbor named Miss Jean.

She was the middle of three children, had a sister one year older and a younger brother. When as young girls Miss Jean and her sister Marian read a book about growing cotton, they begged their daddy for one acre to plant their own crop. He relented and as they planted and tended their field, their mother sat on a blanket with their little brother and watched her independent girls.

During their harvest, she suggested that her young son go and help his sisters. "You always say that you want to be a farmer when you grow up." He took one look at his sisters in a cotton field, pulling bolls and filling bags and said, "I believe I'll be a preacher."

The girls sold their cotton and bought matching wristwatches, my favorite part of that story.

Miss Jean and Miss Marian got college educations because their daddy believed they were just as entitled to a degree as their brother and despite being told he was wasting his money, that the girls should get married and tend to their families, both sisters graduated from Catawba College. They would meet their daddy at the depot in Salisbury, the last stop on his route in the mail car of Southern Railroad, before coming home to Claremont for a few days. He would give them their cash for the week, what was left of his pocket money, and the sisters would go back to the college portion of their lifetime as best friends.

Miss Marian lived with her husband, Mr. Charles, right next door to Miss Jean and her husband Wade. I never knew him. The four of them traveled to the Holy Land and Miss Marian to all fifty states. Miss Jean drew the line after a terrible flight to Alaska and never made it to Hawaii. Or maybe it was the other way around. I can't remember. Either way, she can say she saw 49 states. I get around, but that's more than me. I forgot to count.

Her husband, Wade, came to Claremont as a teacher and saw her playing basketball because, apparently, Miss Jean was a good athlete, and he was smitten. He asked if he could walk her home. She said he could.

They built a pretty brick house and raised two boys. Wade was once elected mayor of Claremont. For rental property, they purchased the house I would eventually buy and it always tickled Miss Jean to see me ripping out ceiling tiles and paneling to get to the original stuff they had spent good money covering up. Wade became good friends with John Busbee and the two of them spent hours on the golf course arguing over the superiority of the University of North Carolina over the University of South Carolina. It was a battle neither won.

Wade would be missing sometimes and Miss Jean would find him on my porch, before it was my porch, sitting in the swing. She recognized that he was not the same man she married, and rarely let him out of her sight. She told me once that he must have realized his mind was betraying him and found comfort in the swing because it looked so much like his homeplace.

After I heard that story I put a swing on the front porch. It comforted me too.

When she needed more help than sons and daughters-in-law could offer, Wade went to live in the Lutheran Home and Miss Jean spent every day there with him. She would kiss him on the forehead before leaving and tell him that she loved him and go home to sleep alone in their pretty brick house.

Mr. Busbee, his good friend and golfing buddy, came to see him one day after Wade had stopped talking or seemed to recognize anyone. Mr. Busbee came because that is what good men do and Mr. Busbee was a very good man. Miss Jean said that Wade looked up to see his lifelong pal standing in the doorway, looked away, and shook his head and spoke for the first time in six months.

"Gamecocks," he said, with disgust.

Miss Jean and I decided we would never fully understand the things men choose to care about.

I know these stories and more because Miss Jean was my neighbor. I would sit on her floor as she got out quilts she sewed and afghans she crocheted and told me of life in Claremont before I knew it. She thought it was funny, and maybe a little profound, that I not only went in The Café but that I sat at the Back Table. "My father would not allow Marian and me to go in there. It was only for men and it wouldn't do for us to be inside." As of her 90th birthday, she had kept to her daddy's rule.

But she ate the cheeseburgers if someone would bring them to her.

Kevin Isenhour and I strong-armed the Appearance Committee into awarding her "Yard of the Month" for her lovely garden of perennials, herbs, and tomatoes. We waited until she went to bed and stuck the sign that declared her the winner right in front of her picture window. When she got up the next morning, she thought someone had put her house up for sale, but laughed and had her picture made with the sign, thrilled at having been chosen.

On Wednesday mornings, I would take her empty trash can back from the street, put it and her recycling tub behind the garage in the little spot of worn, red clay in an otherwise pristine yard. She would see me out in the yard and say, "Why, Shari, I was wondering if you had seen any little trash can fairies out and about because some of them are making sure my trash can gets put back every week?" and I would deny any sightings of magical beings. Occasionally, she would call me and say to meet her on the sidewalk, that since she couldn't properly thank those trash can fairies, she had made a pecan pie for me and hoped I would share it if I saw them. They were roles we continued to play without dropping character. She pretended not to know it was me and I pretended to like pecan pie.

I lost a lot when my house burned. I would have lost more without the solid people of the Claremont Volunteer Fire Department; Catawba, too. I bought new couches and put the family pictures they saved and carried out in new frames. Mike McGraw worked for hours with a soft brush and wax polish on my cowboy boots. I only lost one pair.

When I see Miss Jean, we hug and sometimes we cry, but just a little. If I were a stronger person I would turn down that street and visit her, but I am not, so far, that tough. Haven't been on that road in more than a year. I asked after her and hear that she asks about me.

If I could have just one thing back, it wouldn't be the ceramic horse an old man made for me when I was just a little girl and it wouldn't be the film camera I refused to give up, the one that took pictures of Abbie at balloon races or Walker saving box turtles. I would shrug and give up the Christmas ornaments and the pretty lace dress that an unkind man I had rebuffed said he couldn't believe I even owned.

If I could have one thing back it would be to know that across the street Miss Jean might be reading one of the many books she gets each week from the library, or canning tomatoes from her garden, and that all I have to do is walk out my door and into hers for a good story, a glass of tea, or a slice of pie I don't much care for.

The walk isn't too long and she is there. Maybe this will be the summer I don't see the flames when I look in that direction, don't smell the smoke or hear P.J. Stanley say, "I think it's gone. I am so sorry." Maybe that corner will just be the place where the Saturday night drunks drive into the privet bushes or the best way to get over the railroad tracks without waiting on a train. Maybe it will just be Miss Jean's house I am going to and not a terror I can't quite shake.

I have a lot more land now. I used to have Miss Jean.

ONE TOWN READS ONE BOOK

I thought it was a lack of sophistication, a naivety in how the real world works when I heard them talking in The Café, that they didn't understand the county would never put a library in a town the size of Claremont. I was the one who didn't understand. They may have prayed to a higher power but their real faith was placed in a reluctant mayor and a preacher Colonel.

Margaret Garrison handed me a ticket one morning when I dropped off Walker at school. She said that a Georgia writer was coming to speak in the St. Mark's Church Hall, the only place in town big enough to hold everyone who bought a twenty-dollar ticket for a "Dinner with the Author." Margaret said that I should plan to be there.

It wasn't a request.

Terry Kay came to Claremont. They served Boxcar chicken and mashed potatoes and banana pudding and presented Terry with a bag of socks made at the hosiery mill. After washing the dishes and stacking up the tables and chairs they went right back to wondering how they were going to raise enough money to give the county ten thousand dollars and pay half the salary for a librarian as furniture mills closed their doors for good, and people lost their homes when the fiber optic plant shut down a few short weeks before its first tax bill came due.

Though I had made an appearance at the "Dinner with the Author" and dropped off and picked up Walker daily from the curb of Claremont Elementary I was hiding inside my pretty little house, hiding from myself and everyone else having proven my many critics right, that I could not be trusted to know who to trust. It was safer not to know anyone in my new town other than Margaret Garrison who both terrified and fascinated me as she presided over my son's school in tailored, tasteful suits and seventeen pounds of costume jewelry. Walker referred to her as "the princ-a-bull" and when pointing her out on Kindergarten orientation day had incorrectly but with resolute authority informed me that Scotty Houston her assistant "princ-a-bull," a man twenty-five years her junior was "her husband." Walker was right, though when, his face covered in sauce provided by the PTO welcoming committee at the getting-to-know-you spaghetti supper, he shuddered a little and said, "But, Momma, he is NOT 'the charge'. *She* is 'the charge.'"

I had perfected a ritual of going to The Café to listen without having to talk to anybody, mostly thanks to the cook who manned the grill. He didn't talk to anybody, either and hadn't for the better part of thirty-eight years. There was protocol to ordering at The Claremont Café, a long-standing tradition of standing. You were to stand in line until Jerry Hoke looked at you. When he did it was your signal to order. When he looked away, it meant that he had heard you and you were to go stand somewhere else. The somewhere else was the cement block wall closest to the cash drawer where the bills were piled loosely according to denomination and the change was kept in a butter tub wrapped in duct tape. Jerry's sister, all four feet eleven inches of Miss Janie Edwards would stand from 5:00 a.m. until 2:00 p.m., taking money and yelling orders, "*Cheeseburger All-The-Way!*"/"*Pork Sandwich!*"/"*Bacon, Egg, and Cheese on a Bun!*" or my personal favorite, "*Square Fish and Fries.*" Miss Janie also yelled at her nephew to bring her supplies from the freezer or the back storage room. I would hang around and listen to all the conversations at the tables around me, informed but disconnected until I heard her holler, "*Avery, bring me more tater tots,*" my chosen signal to go home, back to my self-imposed seclusion.

That Jerry didn't talk was legendary. I heard about it in the post office and the grocery store when Claremont finally got a grocery store. To the kids in town he was the weird guy who wouldn't answer when spoken to. To their parents who had grown up going to The Café, first with their parents who still referred to it as "The Pool Room" and later when they met their high school friends for breakfast, Jerry's silence had become an unquestioned part of the experience. It was not, however part of my experience.

Jerry spoke to me.

He didn't chat and he didn't smile but would nod after I said, "Bacon, egg, and cheese, please," more acknowledgement than he had given in anyone's memory. He occasionally gave me sage advice like the day he said, "Quit sayin' 'mayo.' Folks will think yer a Yankee. Just say 'Duke's'." One morning he left his place at the grill when Miss Janie yelled my order, meeting me at her station. As she handed me the plastic basket with the wax paper already soaked in grease Jerry leaned my way and said, "I put an extra piece of bacon on yer sandwich." To all the other patrons of The Claremont Café he remained the guy who didn't write down their orders and flatly refused to speak a word. I wondered how long it would take for me to become just as known for my unwillingness to engage in a town where everyone knew and was most likely related to everyone else.

My resolve lasted through two Christmases and an ice storm. It took pneumonia, a book review, and a NASCAR fan who might have been an angel to break it.

Walker brought a nasty flu home from Margaret Garrison's otherwise safe and peaceful kingdom. On the day he returned to his classroom I came down with the same affliction but with no one to help me, a condition of my own making. The flu brought with it a fever of 102, high enough for me to know that I needed help. I would have to see a doctor where I found myself in an empty waiting room until either a man or, some say a hallucination, came through the door with his arm clutched to his chest.

He wore a plaid shirt with pearl snap buttons and Sans-a-belt pants two inches too short. His white socks peeked from the tops of his patent leather, zipped up, square toed boots. His jet-black hair was slicked back and held in place with pomade and practice, and he topped off this ensemble with a heavy leather jacket embroidered on the back with a giant number "3" and a stitched likeness of the signature of Dale Earnhardt.

49

When the receptionist slid back the window he informed her that he would like twenty dollars worth of medical attention and not a penny more.

"What's wrong with your arm, Roger?" she asked as if she didn't really care. He replied that it was broke. She told him that if it was indeed broke they would have to X-ray it and that alone would eat up his twenty dollars.

"Then, you'd better get it right the first time." he said.

He walked away as she shook her head and shut the window. With a dozen chairs in the waiting room available to him he chose the one across from me and picked up a magazine with his good arm. Evidently, my unfriendly reputation had not reached Roger.

"I seen you looking at my jacket. You a fan?," he asked.

It shocked me, being talked to, being asked a direct question. I shrugged and told him that I didn't really watch racing. He found that both unbelievable and unacceptable.

"But, you know who he is, right? The Man in Black? Number Three? The Intimidator?"

I nodded that I did.

He told me that his car had been broke down when his only child was born, that he had to borrow one to get the baby and his momma home from the hospital. "I made a promise to the boy on that day. I told him, 'Son, this is the last time you'll ever have to ride in a Ford.'"

He asked what was wrong with me, said I sounded awful and that I could have saved myself a whole lot of money had I only called him instead of coming to the doctor because he had a remedy that would fix anything from a steamboat to a broken heart. I smiled because I forgot not to.

It didn't occur to me at the time that Roger was called back to see the doc before I was. I was there first. I was distracted when he handed me a magazine, the one he had clumsily flipped through with his good wrong hand. It was folded back to a page of book reviews.

He said, "Here, you probably like books. You don't have to talk back to them."

There are some who don't believe Roger existed, that it was the fever or the imagination of a would-be writer. I looked for him for a long time but only saw him once after that, after the day he handed me a copy of *People* magazine with a book review I tore from the page and stuffed in my purse, a review that all but dared me to read the book the critic claimed was written by a man "equal to that of the two great Southern writers of our time, Truman Capote and Harper Lee," a review I kept until the fire took it from me.

It took me less than thirty minutes to have the telephone number of a Pulitzer Prize winning writer. The woman at the New York Times was happy to give it to me and told me that he didn't have voice mail but just an "old fashioned answering machine." I left a message. He called me back.

"Shari? This is Rick Bragg. What can I do for you?"

I told him that I lived in a small town in North Carolina where the mayor wanted a library. He said that was a fine thing for a mayor to want. I said that if he would come to Claremont I would organize it so that the whole town would read his book. I would get it in the newspaper and make posters and sell tickets and give all the money to the mayor for his library. Rick said that sounded like fun. "Let's do it" he said. I felt like I must not have made myself clear.

"There isn't any money. To pay you, I mean. There isn't any money."

"I understand." he said.

"I mean, I will buy your plane ticket but there isn't any money for a speaker's fee or anything. There's no money."

"Right. Well, I know how that is."

"I'm saying, I understand how much you probably get to go speak somewhere and there isn't any money for that."

"Yeah, I get it. Do you want me to come or not?"

Rick Bragg gave me his email address and the name and number of a publicist at Knopf who would handle the arrangements. It wasn't until we hung up that I realized I would now have to talk to people in Claremont. During that first phone call to the mayor he wanted to know why he never saw me outside. He was far less interested in what author I could bring to town than he was in my reclusive way of living in his town. He suggested I come to the next "Friends of the Claremont Library" meeting, though there was no Claremont library to befriend, where he pointed out four times in my introduction that he never saw me out in my yard. He said he didn't know this author I could bring to Claremont but he understood he was very popular. A man and his wife at the far end of the table looked at each other. The man spoke.

"He is marvelous, Mayor. Just marvelous. I read his stories in The New York Times and, Miss Smith we are just so honored to have you and so elated that you would go to the trouble of seeking out this wonderful opportunity for us. We would simply love to host another Dinner with the Author for Mr. Rick Bragg."

And I understood. Nothing was decided until Russell Boggs said it was and when he did no one argued. It was in that moment that I was given the gift of acceptance despite not going to church or joining the Lions Club or spending enough time pruning my privet hedge. Before I could leave that meeting I had been invited to four Sunday dinners and promised a pound cake by the weekend.

The next morning I called the *Hickory Daily Record* and lucked into a reporter who wanted the story.

"Rick Bragg is coming to Claremont...? *THE* Rick Bragg? *New York Times* Rick Bragg? Pulitzer Prize winning Rick Bragg? To Claremont...the Claremont with The Café where the guy doesn't talk? *That* Claremont?"

They ran the story on the front page.

The town of Claremont would spend the summer reading *Ava's Man* by Rick Bragg and the author himself would be coming in the fall. They sent a photographer who took a picture of me in The Café with the book on the corner of the table next to a cheeseburger and tater tots. The reporter asked me why I had chosen that book.

I told him that it was the only book I had ever read that deserved to be mentioned in the same breath with *To Kill A Mockingbird*, that it had pissed me off when the critic had written in the review that Rick was equal to Harper Lee and so I had torn the review out of the magazine so I could buy the book, read the book, and write a letter to the critic explaining how wrong he was to cast anyone in the same light.

And, I told him that on page three of *Ava's Man* I knew that I would not write that letter.

The reporter had written that I was pretty the way that Southern women ought to be. On the morning that the story ran Margaret Garrison pulled her white SUV alongside the curb of the sidewalk in front of my house and rolled down her window. "Pretty as Southern women ought to be my ass," she said.

Then she added, "Good job, sweet girl," and drove off.

The citizens of Claremont, North Carolina spent the summer reading *Ava's Man* by Rick Bragg. They had their pictures made with the book, a cashier at the grocery store reading the book with a line of people behind her, a baseball coach with his little league team standing in the dugout looking annoyed, a lady in her flower garden, a teacher at her desk, her students with their hands in the air vying for her attention. They put the pictures on posters and taped them to the windows of the bank and the police department and The Café. They tacked them to the church bulletin boards and sliding glass of the drive-thru lane for paying Claremont water bills. Most all our 1,000 citizens stopped me in the grocery store to tell me stories of their own grandfathers' who had made and sold moonshine and lived lives very similar to that of Charlie Bundrum. Some said that must have been why I thought they would like the book in the first place. One woman told me that Rick's book had given her permission to be proud of her granddaddy, that her family had been ashamed that he couldn't read and got locked up from time to time for the stills he kept flowing in the woods of Catawba County. She said she reckoned that if someone like Charlie Bundrum deserved a book written about him, it was alright for her to be proud of her name and where it came from. We stood and cried together in the dairy section between the eggs and the Cool Whip.

The ladies of The Friends of the Claremont Library formed a committee to make buttons that said, "I've Read *Ava's Man*. Have You?" and passed them out at City Hall to anyone who came in and said they had read the book. I read the book, a chapter every morning to a blind woman who met me at The Café. The Boys at the Back Table would get very quiet. They said it was out of respect, but I knew they were listening to the story. I went to City Hall and got buttons for all of them. They pinned them to their hats and overalls and flannel shirts. Instead of sitting at a table alone and listening to others tell stories, I sat at the Back Table and they almost fought over who got to tell me the next one. Women left casseroles and cherry pies on my porch with thank you notes for introducing them to the book and, for helping to support the effort to bring a library to town.

And fourteen different times I found a copy of *To Kill A Mockingbird* stuck behind the screen door, left there by people who told me that they knew I loved it, that their young'uns had gone off and left it behind, a remnant of their high school English class. They brought them to me either because they thought I did not have a copy of my own or because they knew that there is no such thing as having too many. I'm not sure. I only know that when the fire took my books from me it spared *Ava's Man* and all of my copies of *To Kill A Mockingbird*, including one that

Nelle Harper Lee signed for me when she heard the story of Claremont, the town that read *Ava's Man*.

And, that was the only other time I saw Roger. He came to what was left of my house a few days after the fire to bring me a frozen turkey, said the trucking company he drove for had given to him for Christmas, but he wanted me to have it. He stood there wearing a Dale Earnhardt hat and a T-shirt that read, "Ten Reasons Beer is Better Than Women," holding out the turkey for me to take while Mark Carpenter was helping to carry out what could be saved. I stared at him so long that Mark said, "She ain't herself since the fire, but we sure thank you." And I said, "Mark, can you see him too?"

They sold enough tickets for The Dinner with the Author to fill the church hall. They put oil lanterns on all of the tables in honor of the one Rick's grandmother carried on her lap from house to house when rent money would come due. One of the preachers in town learned to play on his guitar every song mentioned in the book and sang them to us while we ate our Dinner with the Author.

Well, not me. I couldn't eat. I looked out at the room filled with people I had spent too long hiding from. I saw them in their Sunday best, laughing, talking, excited to hear Rick Bragg take the podium, their copies of his books stacked up next to them, waiting on his signature. Rick saw me staring and said, "Are you alright?"

Why don't men know that is as good as opening the floodgates?

I sobbed. I cried and choked and could barely get out the words while Rick sat helplessly wishing he hadn't asked and that I would knock it the hell off. I said, "Look at them. Rick, they didn't know who you were. None of them did. They read that book because I asked them to. I was hiding from these people and now if I so much as sneeze thirteen of them show up with macaroni and cheese."

Rick Bragg said, "Macaroni and Cheese? I would fake a stroke for macaroni and cheese."

That tender moment was clearly over.

He made them laugh, that Dinner with the Author author. I watched them more than I watched Rick. I saw that Tony and Margaret Garrison laugh at the same things and wondered if that was the secret to a strong marriage. Russell said it was "marvelous," but I knew he would both because it was and because he thought everything was marvelous.

54

They wore their buttons and stood in line to get their books signed, and he signed every one of them, that Alabama Writer Boy, and he took the time to talk to them, to my people.

We had a library by the time Rick got to town, a room on the back of City Hall with hand-me-down shelves but a new leather couch that the Mayor got donated by one of our furniture mills.

On the day after the dinner that honored him, I took Rick Bragg to the Claremont Café. He said it was the best cheeseburger he had ever had in his life, and even if that was a lie it was a good lie. The Mayor, and an insurance salesman, and the preacher who sang Big Rock Candy Mountain the night before joined us at our table. I looked up to see Miss Janie coming out from behind the counter. She was carrying a huge, wooden model of a log cabin, nearly too big for her to hold. The Mayor saw her too and asked me what she was doing.

"I don't know," I said. "I've never seen her out from behind the cash drawer. I wasn't sure she even had legs."

She brought the log cabin with real shingles and a chimney covered in tiny rocks over to Rick and handed it to him. He used the table to balance it and looked to me for guidance as to just what was happening.

Miss Janie said, "This is a birdhouse. My brother made it for you," turned around, and walked back to the cash drawer with the duct taped butter tub full of change.

Jerry.

After that everyone in town wanted a birdhouse just like the one he made for that author feller. They placed their orders and he told them when he would have them ready. He had to talk. He came up with new designs, a church, a barn, a barn covered in beer cans, a barn covered in Coca Cola cans, a barn covered in Sundrop cans. He was no longer the strange man who didn't talk.

He was the Bird House man.

More authors came to Claremont. We put up bronze plaques with quotes from their books and the dates of their visits for what we called The Claremont Book Walk. I talked the Boys at the Back Table into going outside to have their picture made with Rick's, a plaque I had insisted be placed as close to The Café as possible. Nine authors came to Claremont. Jerry made a birdhouse for each one of them.

Some years later when we were planning another Dinner with the

Author a reporter wanted to ask Jerry a question for his newspaper story but Jerry wasn't having none of that. I tried and Miss Janie tried but he did not think that thirty-eight years of silence was near long enough when it came to the press and refused to even entertain the idea. He told me to answer for him.

"It doesn't' work like that, Jerry," I told him. "He has to hear you say it to put it in his story."

Jerry wanted to know what it was that the reporter wanted to ask.

I told him it was just one question. "He wants to know why you make a bird house for every author who comes to town."

Jerry said, "I don't do it for them. I do it for you."

Miss Janie shook her head and walked away.

"You oughta knowed that," she said.

KING OF THE WILD FRONTIER

The Chicago Tribune recently allowed three short paragraphs to a story about a police raid in which they confiscated 450 pounds of dried marijuana and 600 live plants. They also found 30 raccoon hides in the freezer. I will bet you a hundred dollars you can't find a Southerner anywhere on the editorial staff of that paper because had that happened below the Mason-Dixon, them boys would have been front page, above the fold.

The first question asked would have been to find out who did the shooting. When they locate that boy, I will post his bail, hand him a 12 gauge, buy him a trailer load of potato chips for the munchies he is bound to have and I will park his ass in a rocking chair on my front porch.

I will sleep like a baby. Ain't like he's gonna miss nothin'.

Think about it. Anyone that baked, anyone that stoned who still has the deadeye aim to kill and freeze the makings of thirty Davy Crockett hats should have movies made in his honor, books written singing the praises of the boy who could shoot straight and roll a fat one at the same time.

This guy should be a legend. Since he's on the run and all, I hope he's headed South where his talents will be fully appreciated.

One morning at the Back Table, Sam said something was growing tall, right straight up in the middle of his hog feed and that he'd been told it was marijuana. The legend that is Gary Sigmon asked him if he smoked it, and I gripped the table for fear he would say that he sure did. But, no, Sam said he let it be, but he said he wouldn't lie and say he'd never tried the real thing. To him, it wasn't all it was cracked up to be. He said it wasn't a bit better than rabbit tobacco.

Gary said he used to work with some boys who smoked before work, during lunch, and immediately after, and he warned them that their lives would be cut short by such foolishness. This advice came from the same man who outran local law enforcement in a '66 gold GTO, once driving home from Salisbury in reverse when his transmission went bad, and got Mike Baker so dead drunk that he tossed him on his bed on a Friday. Baker didn't see daylight again until Monday morning. Gary Sigmon was exactly the one to dispense advice on clean living and healthy habits.

He winked at me when he told this story. Not sure why. Don't much care. I'll take a wink from Gary Sigmon any day—but not a drink.

From across the table Jerry said, "I smoked some once, on the way to the fish camp. Never did find the fish camp."

Bob said that he found what he thought to be an illegal substance in his oldest son's room and decided to find out what all the fuss was about. He told me that he smoked it, "They roll 'em up in paper, you know," and told his wife there was absolutely nothing to it, that a sip of moonshine would do a body more harm than that little cigarette.

She found him sitting on the side of the bed laughing at the television—which wasn't on.

The Chicago Tribune found it necessary to add a line to their story explaining that it was illegal to keep a hide or a carcass thirty days after the season closed.

Yes, with $3.6 million dollars worth of dope, clearly you boys are right to worry about the legalities of raccoon season.

Midwesterners.

When Al Huffman died, the Boys at the Back Table knew he had a case of Mason jars full of white likker. He'd been bragging on it for twelve years. They broke in and found the jars and toted them out as the only item on the menu for their private wake for Al.

Then, they got to thinkin'…

They opened the first jar and smelled it. Nearly took their heads off. A fella they didn't care for was coming down the street. They offered him the first drink. Jerry said he stared straight ahead, stumbled once, and fell over the curb.

They figured that meant it was safe and drank it gone.

I believe that I am the only graduating member of the Class of 1979 who did not smoke dope. It wasn't out of judgment or fear of goin' to hell. It just didn't appeal to me, the look in what was little was visible in my friends' eyes. But I know that a whiskey drunk might break a bar stool over your head while the stoner sitting in the corner is only concerned with peace and love and where he can get a pan of brownies. That's six of one, half a dozen of the other if you ask me.

I am wasting my time at this keyboard. I need to find Bob's son and asked him if he's been spending any time in Chicago.

DESIGNING WOMEN

Miss Maebelle and Miss Glenna Mae are best friends.

They come in The Café for lunch most days except Friday, which anybody with good sense knows is their day at the hairdresser's. If you see one, you see the other. I've heard them argue over which one cusses the most, a debate that ended when Maebelle said that she only cussed when she drank and since her stomach went bad, she isn't allowed to drink therefore she does not cuss. Miss Glenna Mae said she never did do no damn cussin'.

They've been neighbors since Johnson was President. Their husbands have passed. They go to the same church, St. Mark's Lutheran on Main Street, the one on the right if you're facing north and confused by two Lutheran churches built right next to one another in a town of less than one thousand people. They travel a good bit, go to the beach or the mountains where they got snowed in for a solid week. The Boys at the Back Table laughed and laughed about how funny they thought it was that Maebelle and Glenna Mae were stuck up there in the mountains, in some log cabin, with not one thing to do but talk to each other.

I knew better.

We grow up learning about the rise and fall of the Roman Empire and all the stupid things men did that messed up a perfectly good world domination. We're taught the proper placement of a comma and not to dangle a participle, though I think commas are pretty and will use them anywhere I damn well want to. Just ask my editors if I won't. The well meaning school systems of this country will even waste everybody's time teaching math, a subject I have managed to either avoid or decimate for going on fifty years, so you tell me I should have paid more attention in Mrs. Balser's class.

But not once, in being told how to mix up biscuits with a fork or to abstain from canning tomatoes if "Aunt Sally" was visiting, ('cause the lids won't seal), not once did anyone tell me how much I would need my girlfriends.

I should have picked it up from watching old women, but I was young and stupid and more interested in what those good looking boys were thinking. I found out, much of the time, they ain't.

I know a lot of good men, fine men, men who would take a bullet for me. Some of them are educated and well-read and some of them are neither and one of them can't write more than his own name, but they are good and honest and I love them, I love them true. But I know that when life falls apart, you need your girls.

When my sweet Labrador puppy died from an ugly disease left in my yard by a pack of strays, my next door neighbor, the former mayor of this fine town, was all but loading the gun for an evening of stray dog killin', despite the fact that he'd be breaking several city ordinances and state laws. His wife, she came over and sat in my kitchen and talked.

And laughed. And cried.

When my house was on fire and sending black smoke into the sky, Robin McGraw got in her car, drove into town and threatened the man parts of the boys at the barricades. She said she was coming through and they said yes ma'am. She was crying before she hugged me but she soon wiped her eyes and got on her cell phone and barked orders at people for the next two weeks. My son had an emergency wardrobe before they had put out the flames. When volunteers, through charred ceiling beams and soaked insulation, found their way to his closet, she had women all over Catawba County washing his clothes the way *she* said to do it; spray with

Febreeze, hang outside, wash twice with Gain detergent and dry with two dryer sheets. If they still smell, throw them out. Robin worked until she saved two quilts my grandmother sewed from patches of my aunts' dresses and my dad and granddaddy's work shirts.

How are you supposed to thank somebody for that?

Alisa Carpenter stood up front with me the morning after, when I went to the churches. It's the most efficient way of communicating with people of Claremont. I was wearing a coat someone had wrapped around me the night before and hadn't brushed my hair or washed my face. I spoke but I remember little of it. I explained that it started with a wood cookstove and that we wouldn't know what we needed for several days but I sure did appreciate how much everybody wanted to do. Most of that week is a blur. They say I had a conversation with Jeff Murray when he offered to send over his crew to help carry, and with D.B. Setzer about bringing over a tractor trailer to use for storage, but I have no memory of it. I do remember Alisa, standing behind me in the church, her hands clasped in front of her and tears falling, soft sobs in the background while I talked.

It was the last time I saw her cry.

She carried out and washed and scrubbed every dish and pot and pan and this and that we could find and she found more than anyone else would have. She organized an army of strong boys in their twenties to carry what she couldn't and made decisions she knew I was, at the time, incapable of making. When she found me one morning, sitting in my truck, sobbing uncontrollably, she opened my door and looked at me. I was so thankful she was there, believed she would wrap her arms around me and understand how awful it was, cry with me in the aftermath of the worst thing that had ever happened to me.

Instead, Alisa smiled from ear to ear and said, "Now, what am I gonna do with you? Come on, and hear Katie practice. She's singin' a solo at church on Sunday morning. You should come but you won't."

I stopped crying and went to choir practice.

Edie Connor fixed baked spaghetti and put makeup in a little basket by the sink on my first night in the borrowed apartment. She said to call her if I needed her but she was leaving because my boy and I needed some time to ourselves to talk and work all this out of our systems.

She did the dishes, too.

Years before, when I saw no way out of a relationship that all but killed me, Margaret Garrison looked me in the eye and told me, "It's time, sweet girl. It is time. You have to go and you have to go now." And she was right. She always is. Take Julia Sugarbaker, throw in an occasional swearing and big, gaudy, tacky costume jewelry and you have The Great Margaret Garrison. Once we were talking about grown children when Margaret said, "They do not need to think for themselves until I am dead."

If you knew her, you would agree.

I had good girls before I came to Claremont though I am ashamed of the bad job I did in fully appreciating them. Marla Jones could drive the getaway car full of girls hoping to avoid prosecution and graduate in 1979 faster than any boy in the county, and she did it with eyelashes Hollywood would die for. The girl knew mascara and how to make full use of a gas pedal. I can still hear her sweet voice as she threw Levis at my head on those Saturday mornings right soon after McDonalds had come out with a new item on the menu, "Shit! Get up and get in the car or we're gonna be too late for Egg McMuffins!" Driving fast while applying eye makeup was but one of her many gifts.

Sometimes Paula Schroeder was in the car with the rest of the criminal element but more often she was an Accessory After the Fact. Paula was born maternal, destined to be a caretaker. She babied a football player who did not deserve her and doted on Andy Smith, her childhood best friend. She baked cookies and soothed broken hearts and she married the cutest boy, Rich Hawkins, a year behind us in school.

My own Abbie would soon be a year old the day I got the phone call that Paula's baby boy had been born and was in trouble. I dropped Abbie off with a sitter and flat flew to the hospital. Baby Quinton was gone before I got there. Paula's mother and sister, Beth, were in her room, guarding her like German Shepherds. The men were standing in the hallway. Paula told me Quinton had dark hair and looked like Rich. That next summer when we sat on bleachers and watched grown men play softball like it was the World Series and winning meant rings and ticker tape parades, Paula said, "You know, you are the only one who talks about him, about Quinton. Everyone is afraid to mention it. They act like he wasn't here but he was. He was to me."

Me, too.

Paula has four of the prettiest children, even if three of them are boys, and three pretty grandbabies even if all of them are boys. They pile on top of each other for pictures she posts on Facebook and look like a wacky bunch only found in 50's television families. Paula is always smiling.

Paula Schroeder Hawkins is the mother of five babies, not four, and we remember that. We remember him, her girlfriends, her partners in crime.

There are a hundred ways to measure friendship, yardsticks to use when choosing the label "Best Friend." I often say that if I ever need to bury a body I will call Alisa Carpenter. That body would be six feet in the clay and she would be back to cookin' ham and beans before they realized anybody'd gone missing. But, truth is, I have always had an army of gravediggers, women who will sacrifice their time and bail money to come running if I need them. One of them is a corporate giant in St. Louis who calls me on long drives. One is living with a rock star in L.A., taking pretty pictures and partying with famous people and still checks my blog every day. One of them is only three hours away, telling me daily that I'm good at this writing thing when I am pretty sure the jury is still out. One of them, Lady Blue, out there on the coast, I've never met, but she is there; don't think for a minute she ain't. Another, who writes dark and stormy books, even lives in Alabama. Who would think a Carolina girl could find anything divine among Tigers and Crimson? *Roll Tide, my ass...* but, there she is, writing like a fallen angel with her cigarette and "little whiskey drink." They are my girls, scattered like Steel Magnolias, gathered like hoop skirts and pinafores.

When your house burns or your dog dies or your boyfriend is Satan or Keith Whitley drinks himself to death, (lord, that was a bad day), the men go to pacing, trying to figure out what to do, what to say.

But, women just know. I do believe we are designed that way.

HARMLESS LIES, POETRY AND CHEESEBURGERS ALL THE WAY

In Claremont, love of the hunt and its traditions is the tie that binds men and memories.

I don't keep up with decisions made by the boys in Raleigh as to deer season. When I come down the hill, ease over the railroad tracks, and through my windshield see the finest people I know gathered around the bed of a pickup truck parked behind the bank across from the Claremont Café, I know the season opened on Saturday morning. They will have left grits and eggs waiting on the tables to come and stand, staring down, their hands shoved in the pockets of their camouflage coats or bib overalls, their shoulders pulled up to their ears to keep the cold from their necks. They will remark on size and age, ask as to location and time, remember aloud their own hunts long ago or the morning before, and I will know that a deer is dead and it is worthy of a viewing.

The hand painted sign out front says Claremont Café, but to locals it's The Pool Room, though there hasn't been a game of eight ball played there since 1970. It's where we go in this small Carolina town to stay up on news and eat grease the surgeon general swears will kill us all. Once a mule was ridden in one door and out the other, and there was also an unsolved robbery when someone stole the stovepipe. Never bothered to call the law. There is the occasional arms deal at the Back Table, and handmade skinnin' knives are often being admired at the counter. You don't have to be armed to eat there, but it's not an altogether bad idea.

Bob Winstead will unbutton the top of his blue jeans before he sits down to eat gravy and toast. As thin as Bob is and has always been, a meal at The Café can test the strength of denim. So tiny he has carried the nickname of PeePee—no bigger than a baby chicken—since his working days in the furniture mills of Catawba County, Bob sits every morning at a table with Gary Sigmon, and with his wife since she retired. If Bob is missing, he's off hunting. In days long past, Gary Sigmon outran the law in a gold '66 GTO, brought an insurance company to its knees with a can of spray paint and survived a near death experience involving a septic tank and a John Deere, yet eagerly awaits Bob's return, knowing there might be a good story to hear. Bob Winstead has always hunted, always fished, and always worked. Retirement brought freedom to his schedule but little opportunity for porch sitting. He helps a brother with a broke-down engine or a son crossing his heart and swearing he does not know how that hole got in his daddy's boat.

Bob and his sons put venison and fish in the freezers and on the dinner plates of neighbors all over Claremont, including my own. I've opened my door to find him standing over a cooler, offering enough to feed an army if I am willing to cut up and wrap, and I always am. He once belonged to a hunting club, a group of ten or so, but now hunts with his boys, Robbie and Kelly, in the pines of Catawba County and just across the line into Virginia, their get-gone for the past some years. They hunt deer and turkey when the seasons allow and fish the rest of the time. Ask Bob if there is anything he always wanted to hunt but didn't and his answer will be a wink and a smile and a draw on his pipe. "Yeah," he'll say, "but I forgot her name."

C-3, called so for the Charles Connorses who came before him, will be on a Naugahyde stool at the counter, and we'll all be sworn to secrecy as to his presence, cholesterol, and his wife's concern for his longevity.

He named his 300 acres Wood Duck Bend for the daily flight pattern of those birds from Lyle Creek to his pond. A hen made a home in his wood stove before he could get a cap on the chimney, or a fire lit in the cabin he built there close enough to hear the water running over rocks and around a beaver dam. It wasn't family who brought him to the hunt but rather John Busbee and Roland Pope. C-3 walked the railroad tracks that cut through town with Mr. Busbee and his dogs when the broom straw was thick with coveys of quail, and rabbits ran in every direction, lining up birds on a bale of straw in the back of his '78 Audi. The car, the quail, and the old men are gone now. Mr. Busbee, a man so kind and good to people that he was forgiven for having been born in South Carolina, was fond of saying that young men hunt behind pointers and old men hunt over setters. We would see him at lunch time ordering cheeseburgers to go, taking them back to his corner drugstore, where in retirement he sat near the door and talked to folks coming in for prescriptions or birthday cards. His great-grandchildren are now learning the Busbee tradition of quail and grits and eggs on Christmas morning, and memories of Irish setters that were so much more than pretty redheads.

Mr. Busbee's favorite story was of traveling east near Statesville with C-3 and a borrowed dog not worth the time it took to feed him. With no quail and a sorry dog, the men were offered another dog, a better dog, and used him to find every bird in Iredell County. At the end of a day saved by a good nose, C-3 wanted to buy him. He wasn't for sale at any price they were told by their host, the owner of the dog. "Aw, everybody's got a price," reasoned C-3, "and I'm willing to pay it." The man refused his offer of $200, then $300, and C-3, a man not partial to "no," offered another $100. The man thought for a minute and said he sure did hate to do it but if C-3 was willing to part with $400 for a dog he'd only seen hunt one time, well then, he reckoned he would sell him, and C-3 nodded his head in the self-assured, damn-right confidence of a man who could buy most anything he wanted. He turned to Mr. Busbee and said, "Uh, John, you got any cash? I left mine back in Claremont," and for the 30 minutes it took to get home, Mr. Busbee owned a Brittany spaniel.

Some folks see dollar signs when looking at C-3, and it's true that his checkbook can buy him duck hunting in Alaska and Arkansas, where he swears they are lying about ivory-billed woodpeckers, and he's got himself a gas-guzzling, dually truck and a shiny Breitling watch. But that same checkbook paid for the fancy bus with soft seats that took us on the four hour drive to cheer for the varsity girls' basketball team that earned a spot in the regional championship game, and every now and then it answers a phone call from John Busbee's son at the drugstore when someone can't afford pills that keep a heart pumping good. Besides, C-3 knows that Breitling doesn't keep a bit better time than Bob Winstead's Timex. He just likes pretty things. It's why he married Edie.

His boy, C-4, chooses to sit at the Back Table with men much older than his 20 years. He plants food crops for deer and turkey and tends to the wood duck boxes he has placed around the creek. He's determined to replenish the quail population of Catawba County by his own hand, calling his daddy from the pen to remind him of the need for another heat lamp. He spends as much time on a John Deere as he does in a study group at Appalachian State, eager to be back in a deer stand or duck blind. On the morning after Thanksgiving, his seventh grade year, the deer that would be his first stood within range as his daddy motioned for him to shoot. So nervous he believed the deer could see his breath, he decided to hold it until the deer was down, only it was C-4 who was down when he passed out due to lack of oxygen and fell to the floor of the stand. The deer splashed into the water of Lyle Creek, while C-3 said, "Give me the gun, son," and spine-dropped him. Pulling the boy to his feet, he handed him the gun and said, "I think I missed. Get him before he gets gone," as C-4 shot a dead deer. One of them believes it to be a tale of what fathers do for their sons, and another believes his daddy stole his first deer.

C-4 will get his degree in risk management and insurance and sit at a desk at the family business because he has a sense of his privilege, that his was a childhood without worries about final notices from Duke Power or if the mill would lay off his momma or daddy, and he is grateful for it. He will take his place in a line of good businessmen, smart businessmen, because he can, because it is what is expected, because he is thankful for the blind luck of his birth. But it's not what he wants. Charles Connor the Fourth wants to farm. He wants to walk the red clay of Catawba County and look to the sky for rain or sun. He wants to stand just below the pines and hear quail call, quail he has nurtured with sorghum crops and cover until his 100 acres are full enough to provide for his supper.

C-4 wants to spend his days free from the chain of a computer screen and oxford cloth shirt, and ride in his pickup truck with the window down, the wind blowing back the sleeve of his Wing Shooters T-shirt on his way to the kennel. He wants to see if Labrador puppies were born in the night, before coming to The Café for breakfast, and to talk to the other farmers, the men who are free.

Glen Overcash will be at the Back Table with the others who have earned the privilege of sitting at Claremont's prime spot for harmless lies. Glen has always reminded me of a '50s movie star, the handsome loner who tips his hat and is gone, leaving heartbroken women standing in the dust. I half expect to see him ride in on a pretty paint horse and place six-shooters on either side of his livermush and egg plate. Sometimes he is gone for a good bit, hunting in Halifax County where he'd just as soon cook for his buddies as hunt. Glen Overcash can fix the grill at The Café, making him the most important man in Claremont. He and I nearly died laughing the day a belly dancer came sashaying in for the 75th birthday of Sam Willis. There's a picture of it—Sam, his wife and daughters, and a half-nekked belly dancer—stuck to the wall with black electrical tape. That was a good day.

Mike Benfield will be there, too, at that Back Table. Nobody's man enough to take his chair. Benfield fills up a room, seems bigger than he is and he's plenty big enough. He knows the river, every bend, every branch of the Catawba, grew up there with a history deep in Catfish—the fire district, not the bottom feeder. He is a deer hunter and a hard worker and a fine friend who will not sell me his 1950 Chevy truck no matter how many real tears I manage to work up. He claims he learned to drive it before he was big enough to reach the pedals but that's a lie. There never was such a time.

Jim Bryant warrants a place at the Back Table, but sometimes chooses the counter. He has an encyclopedic knowledge of Catawba County history and a talent for explaining to tree huggers that they are late to the party, that farmers and hunters were the first environmentalists. As his children grew, Jim purchased five identical Ruger rifles to match his own longtime favorite, proof that he knows what does and does not matter. The first one was for a son turning 12, the second to replace the first after Jim left it on the cab of his truck and drove away; the third was the reward he offered for the first which he kept seven years for the next boy in line, the fourth for the next son who turned 12, and the fifth when his only daughter graduated from college.

I heard Jim talking one day about mounts, the why of stuffing things killed in the woods and sticking them on a nail pounded in the dining room wall. Jim Bryant painted a prettier picture than writers who have been trying to capture it for decades.

He was talking to the younger hunters and said that he doesn't tote a deer head to a taxidermist to feed his own ego, but to recall the battle, the grace and fight in the buck, the worthiness of his opponent. "When someone comes into my house for the first time, I point to one and tell his story, remember every sound and smell, and never do I claim it as a victory, his death. I only seem to recall how many times he evaded me." It sounded, for all the world, like poetry.

The Sigmon family takes up a whole table, though usually there are chairs holding up the backsides of several others, not kin, gathered around, laughing like fools. The Sigmon brothers were born over a span of 25 years, the youngest, Stan, at 46, losing his father before he turned 16. It was Joe and Ted, one gone, the other now 66, who put a gun in his hand and squared him toward a running rabbit. For overnight hunts they rigged the back of a pickup with plywood and sleeping bags so they could double the room, sleep six to a truck. The guy on the top level, closest to the tailgate, would have to open the door of the camper shell in the mornings and lift on the handle so the guy on the lower bunk could ease down the gate, but that's not the only example of their resourceful nature.

One member of their hunting party had taken a shotgun along on a deer hunt in case there were no deer but plenty of waterfowl. He saw a pair of wood ducks over the flooded timber of the Roanoke River and dropped them both. The problem with dropping ducks on a deer hunt is the sorry lack of retrieving dogs or proper waders, and so an abandoned washtub became a makeshift boat. He was a slight man, less than 130 pounds, but turns out washtubs aren't as much for keeping a man dry as they are for keeping his beer cold, and midway between land and ducks, he started to sink. More compassionate friends would show sympathy when telling of a buddy who nearly froze, but the Sigmon boys laugh until tears roll and claim that it's fine because, "He didn't die or nothing." No one remembers if he got his ducks.

Stan owns a landscaping company and without much yard mowing or shrub pruning after November, Stan Sigmon hunts. He knows where the deer hide, where the sweet spot is for ducks along Lyle Creek, and if he was more of a selfish man he'd keep that information to himself. He has trained his second dog now, a lab named Drake that circles once before delivering to hand, but there seems little need to fix that and so they hunt ducks with Stan's son, Josh, and any friend with a license who comes along.

Josh dropped a deer some years ago in Bertie County hunting with his daddy and Jeff Bolick. It was dark by the time they went back to get the deer, and Stan, several yards ahead, radioed to Jeff and Josh that a bear had beaten them to it. He could see eyes in the glow of his flashlight and realized his tragic mistake, leaving the gun behind. "He's circlin' me, boys. Stay where you are." They would all learn a valuable lesson that day about leaving guns locked in the cab of a truck, and Stan would learn a thing or two about hunting with Jeff Bolick. When the warning came over the radio, Jeff said, "Let's go, Josh. No sense in all of us gettin' eat."

Josh waited on his daddy.

Josh Sigmon is the best young man I know, and I embarrass him as often as possible by telling him so. Some folks are born good. They grow good and the good of them lasts into forever. You can just tell. This past Fourth of July he pulled at me when the DJ fired up a sweet song by the Van Zandt boys, the one telling Mr. Young his presence is not required in the South, and I danced with a good-lookin' boy barely legal for the first time in close to 30 years. Josh prefers to duck hunt, but is in the hay fields during dove season and in a tree stand when allowed by law. This year, he applied for his first tundra swan permit. I sure hope he gets a bird. I sure do.

His Uncle Ted is really more a grandfather to him and tortures the boy in ways only grandfathers are allowed. Ted is a cattle farmer, spends early mornings crunching frost under his feet while he checks on the young ones, the ones due any day, and when he can't or won't go hunting with Stan and Josh, he calls their cell phones to get the count. Stan said, "Even if we haven't hit a thing, I tell him' 'We're stackin' 'em up like cord wood.'"If they went home empty-handed, they claimed to have left some for seed.

Ted knows they're lying and gets even by dropping deer on days the younger generations never see one. To Jason Carpenter, a family friend, this is particularly irritating. His daddy didn't teach him to hunt. Ken

Carpenter would rather be brushing the cockleburs from the tail of a brood mare, so Jason taught himself to use a bow and spends a fair amount of time hunting with the Sigmons. "I bought every piece of equipment they make, the base layer, scent block shirts and pants and jackets, and I even got a pair of them 1,000 gram boots. Ted walks in the woods with blue jeans and that same tan jacket he wears every day, and a pair of white-damn-tennis shoes and kills a buck." Ted tells Jason that his money's been wasted. "I spit on their backs when they walk under my tree stand. It don't bother them."

It is often the Sigmon Landscaping truck I see parked behind the bank, admirers peering over the side. They tend to bring them to The Pool Room before putting them in the freezer. Josh told me once that it is part of their tradition, letting everyone have a look. "Yeah, if it's a good one, one worth showing off, Dad will say, 'Let's ride him around till he rots.'"

David Carpenter is likely to pull a chair up to the Sigmon table. David graduated from Bunker Hill High School with a 3.8 GPA, a gold tassel, and two awards for top rifleman in the district. He started with a Chipmunk .22 and a squirrel in his own back yard after which his momma took his picture and stuck it in his baby book with photographs of missing teeth and first haircuts. Most of the birthdays and Christmases of his 20 years have brought a gun, appreciation for firearms a part of his family. His momma, my best-good girl friend, and I were shopping one day last summer for cute shoes and silver bracelets. I was trying out a new shade of lipstick when she asked if we had time for a quick stop. "I need to run by and pick up my concealed carry permit. Gotta stay legal!"

David was born an old man. He frets and worries over things and will squeeze a nickel till it squeals, but he paid cash for his shiny pickup and his four-wheeler and has earned his reputation as a hard worker. A woman from a local furniture mill, working in the sewing room with his mamaw, saved her husband's guns for 15 years after he died, knowing her children would sell them with no thought to their time on the shoulder of a hunter. Upon his graduation, she laid them before David and told him to take his pick. He chose well, a Browning A5, with engraving and a smooth walnut stock, the gun of a real bird hunter, and so it hunts again, serves another good man.

David hunts doves and ducks with Josh Sigmon, but he hunts deer with his Uncle Brian. Brian's grandfather, Floyd Gantt Sr., took him on his first hunt, had him lay out of a day of second grade to hunt over on River Bend Road because by that time, the die was cast. When he was three, Brian's momma had bribed him to stop sucking his thumb with the promise of a BB gun, a promise she made good on. He rushed the mailbox with that BB gun one day when an 8-point buck stood eating the acorns that had fallen around it.

He missed.

Brian hunted rabbits and squirrels on his own, but trailed his grandpa and well-bred pointers and setters through pines so high they disappear in blue sky. Paw Gantt believed a man should hunt every day and was ill with Brian when girls and cars took a place among his interests. He needn't have worried. Brian Hefner would hold to the belief that a man belongs in the woods. He would be with David when at age 12, he got his first deer, take him to HG and H Bait Shop to have his picture made and put on the wall, and he would provide for his aging grandfather the same opportunity.

Brian hauled slabs to the woods and built a blind on the ground so an old man wouldn't have to climb, one that would keep the wind from his grandfather, allowing him to stay in the woods all day if he wanted. Inside, he placed a sturdy chair with a thick cushion and hung an extra coat on the wall. He kept apples and other snacks close by in case his grandfather took hungry waiting on his trophy buck.

Floyd called Brian at work one day and said to come on home, he needed help with a deer. Brian thought he was to go to the woods, but Floyd Gantt had wrestled the buck into the trunk of his LTD and brought it on to the house. "I got him in, but I can't get him out."

Floyd was 88 years old.

Brian helped him but not before he took him to HG and H, the same as he had for his nephew, got his picture made and put it on that famous bulletin board. He took his grandfather home and cleaned the deer, put the meat in the freezer, and made one more stop before going to bed. Brian Hefner went back to the woods, back to the deer stand and picked up the shell casing, a 30.06, and put it in his pocket. It has been with him every day since then and was in his pocket the day they buried his grandfather, a year ago this January. He was 97.

There may come a day when I can't keep up with the light bill, but I will never go hungry. The men in my life are hunters. They are my family, though I am not blood kin to any one of them. Some say it is the way of a small town, but that's not always so. It is so in Claremont. If there was ever any doubt it burned away on a gray day last November when my pretty little house with the wrap around porch and fishscale shingles sent black smoke into the sky. Some shed their camo and donned the coats of the volunteer fire department to fight back the flames with hoses and hatchets. When Gary Sigmon got the call he rushed to my side so fast he didn't hang up the phone before grabbing the truck keys and yelling at his wife to "come on." We stood on the hill and watched it burn. Gary never spoke a word. In one hand he held the ever present cigarette and in the other he held onto me. The toughest man I know cried that day. I won't soon forget that.

In the days after the fire, the men of the Claremont Café shoved paper money in my hand and issued warnings not to trust insurance folk. The young boys carried out what they could and didn't talk much. When there was nothing more to save they looked at their own boots, shifting from one to the other, soot and ashes temporarily taking from them their youth and laughter. Months later they joked and taunted each other with claims of superior strength as they backed their pickups to a new porch and unloaded furniture, some new, some restored, stopping to listen for gobblers in the woods that now surround me. The old men tell me stories that connect me to the history of the new place in the same way they made me proud to live in the one now gone, and try their damnedest to tell me what to do.

They argue over the best way for me to feed deer and turkey and called me "hardheaded" when I took to painting my barn with a brush. They volunteered to run off a worthless man and threatened to disown me if I didn't make an effort to hang onto a good one. They are my family, my daddies and granddaddies, my brothers, my own young'uns. They are my heavenly band full of angels, come to keep me close and set me free. They wear the clothes of working men who dip snuff and cuss like it's an art, and when it comes their time, St. Peter will know he's lucky to have them and that there will be no dragging me through those pearly gates if they aren't there. Better someone ride me around till I rot.

Things change, the way we listen to music, the shows on television, and for me, the direction I turn on my way to the Claremont Café. But if it's not Ted or Stan Sigmon it will be Josh and someday it will be Josh's own boy showing off when I see the gathering, men looking down into the bed of a pickup truck, and I will know that the season started on Saturday morning, that a deer is dead, and is worthy of a viewing.

MATTHEW

Walker had fretted most of the afternoon.

He was a card-carrying member of the National Honor Society, a piece of lamination that cost me eighty bucks. He carried all A's the last semester of his Junior year, could list the presidents, the endangered species list, and every statistic of the Tar Heels, a trait that had made me consider jumping from a moving vehicle on most road trips lasting three hours or more. But on that day he was certain he had failed his algebra exam.

He didn't.

It was official. Walker was a senior and it was the summer before his last year of high school. When the house burned, Walker told me he wanted two things; a real Christmas, free of being those sad people who lost their home, and to graduate with his friends. Most of them began kindergarten with him and I have to look real hard not to see them that way now, five-year-olds whom all of us, their mommas, shared in a way. They were our sweet little boys and we forever shunned the woman who said that Cole McGraw "was as mean as a snake."

On that day, I got to thinking back over the last twelve years, remembering the time Walker threw up in the McGraws' car and the time Cole threw up in mine. There is the unforgettable, fall down laughing kind of funny story on Jeremy Null known as "the Munchos Incident," but that is for another time. Phillip Hicks, a seventeen-year-old so good that even his buddies try not to cuss in his presence, slipped off that pedestal long enough to cut the hair of his third grade teacher when she leaned over his desk. Phillip had his picture taken that year wearing a T-shirt that read, "Future President of the United States."

He might could be.

They picked up one or two along the way, good boys, all of them, athletes, most of them, and they remained good friends without blood drawing brawls. They were to graduate together a year from then, mortar boards and college acceptance letters scattered around them with a week's worth of dirty laundry and gym bags no one with a good sense of smell would go near.

Only one of them was missing.

Mary Anne Schoener called late one afternoon in the spring of their freshman year.

Her name on Caller ID was enough to make me afraid of the phone, of that call. Her son, Matthew, and Walker ran up the sidewalk together into their first day of kindergarten, stood next to each other as they sang loudly and badly in their first grade Christmas pageant, and played against each other the summer before their second grade year when Matthew's yellow soccer team beat the pants off Walker's red soccer team. Walker was the goalie.

Before school could start that fall, before they would be eight years old, Matthew would be diagnosed with MLD, a form of dystrophy I never could pronounce. He started second grade using a walker, needed a wheelchair for their October trip to the zoo, and by the end of the year could remember that his favorite race car driver was Jeff Gordon, but didn't recognize his number when looking at a flash card showing him "24."

He wasn't talking to us anymore by the start of third grade, but his parents brought him to school every day having been told he could last no more than two more years. They wanted him to be around other children, to hear them, because by the fourth grade, Matthew was blind.

The kids fought over who got to push his wheelchair, and unbelievably, who got to wipe his chin. They read to him, teased him about girlfriends, and threatened to put snakes in his backpack because long after he didn't talk, Matthew Schoener could laugh. They understood feeding tubes and private nurses and they learned empathy from a boy who used to run faster than most of them.

Matthew made it past his two year prediction and the third and on and on, going to school whenever possible, parked in the back of a room full of cheerleaders and ballplayers, kids who patted him and spoke when they went to their next class. We cried with his momma when she needed us to and sometimes when she wasn't looking and we prayed, all of us, first that the doctors had gotten it wrong, then that Richard and Mary Anne could find a way to cope, and selfishly, we sent private prayers of thanks that it was not our own boy. Richard and Mary Anne probably knew that and didn't hold it against us.

Matthew was still here for the beginning of high school with the class of 2011.

The boys at my house that day, the evening she called, came to watch the Final Four. Jeremy had just the day before pitched a perfect game and would accept a full ride to play baseball for Western Carolina and be drafted by the Seattle Mariners. Nick Isenhour, a football player and wrestler, was ranked 5th in their class at the time. He won a Pre-Cal award, a Presbyterian College Achievement Award, and a place at Boys State. They were awash in a sea of Carolina Blue when I walked into the living room, ready for the game as all fifteen year olds in the state of North Carolina should have been.

None of them declined to go to Matthew's house to say goodbye.

They washed the Carolina Blue paint from their faces, took off the Styrofoam fingers and raided Walker's closet and dresser drawers for more appropriate things to wear, as if there is anything appropriate about teenage boys going to see a friend for the last time.

They stood around Matthew, his body drawn up, unable to relax now for so long. On the car ride to the Schoener's, Nick asked me, "What do you say to someone who is dying?" and the other boys joined in, worried they would say or do the wrong thing and upset his parents. They didn't believe me when I told them they would know what to do.

Mary Anne apologized to them for interrupting their game. "We don't know how long it will be, guys. We sure appreciate you coming and believe that Matthew knows you are here." Walker asked her if she remembered that he used to draw Matthew a picture every day in second grade, an eight-year-olds' attempt to make it all better, a piece of Crayola art, his impressions of snakes or spiders or dinosaurs, critters he knew Matthew liked. Tears flooded her eyes and Mary Anne said, "I still have every one."

On that day, I watched each of the boys in men's bodies pat their buddy on his bended knee as we said, "Bye, Matthew." "See ya, dude." "Later, Matt." His mother smiled and thanked them by name, one after the other. I had taken a copy of *To Kill a Mockingbird*, held it in my hands for reasons I cannot explain and when it was my turn, I whispered things that will remain between me and Matthew.

In less than an hour they were back in my living room, ready for the game. No one repainted his face. No one put the Ram Horns back on his head.

Jeremy came in the kitchen and asked me how long it would take, how long before we'd get another call, and I told him there was no telling. He looked down at me, for the boy who was a kindergartner a very little while ago was by then over six foot five. "Do you think he will make it to the end of the game?"

And in that moment I saw our little boys, our five-year-olds, but did not trust myself to speak, to answer him. Jeremy said, "I guess you're right. There's no tellin', huh?" And to this day, I don't know how I lived through that.

Mary Anne called again to ask if Walker would mind being a pall-bearer. We got him a new suit and the only pair of size fifteen dress shoes in Hickory. He worried that he would not do everything he was supposed to do, stand when he was supposed to stand, kneel when the Catholics went to their knees, but it was my son-in-law, twelve years Walker's senior, who said it perfectly. "Walker never disappoints us."

The Great Margaret Garrison spoke at the funeral. It was the only time I ever saw her have to *try* to be the rock we needed her to be. She steeled herself and spoke of Richard and Mary Anne's dedication to getting Matthew to school every day he was able, the work of bathing and dressing and loading a wheelchair into a van, only to come a few miles for a few hours. She thanked them for that and when she did I had to hold steady to the church pew. She smiled at the Schoeners, thanked them for the lessons Matthew had taught our children, thanked them for the lessons they had taught us, thanked them for allowing her to be Matthew's principal, as if anyone else would have fought that hard to get what he needed to be in a classroom, and because I could not take my eyes from her, I saw it. I saw Margaret Garrison gather herself, summon the strength to walk off the altar. She had nothing left.

I wasn't sure that was possible.

I watched my son carry his childhood friend. Matthew was dressed in sweat pants and the T-shirt of his favorite morning radio deejays. I watched his mother smile at my son, forever the nurturer—she was letting him know he was doing fine and later, when I stood by her at the cemetery, after the doves and balloons were released, after the mourners had run out of things to say, I commented that we were both wearing brown. Mary Anne said, "I borrowed this from Natalie. Can you believe they wanted to take me shopping for a dress to wear to my son's funeral? I don't want the dress I would wear to my son's funeral."

And we cried. We laughed a little, too.

I always thought about Mary Anne at the milestones our boys reached. I hope she knows that. She recorded every school assembly, every Christmas concert, every field day. I missed seeing her, always in shorts and a T-shirt even when I was neck deep in flannel and goose down. She was busy with their Jenny, busy being her mom, but Jenny was too much younger to be at the same school events. We found out that there's a lifetime between middle and high school.

Mary Anne told me once that when she drove past my house, when she saw the cars parked down at the barn, the lights on, when she saw those boys playing basketball together as high schoolers just as they had as first graders, she knew that Matthew would have been with them. She said it made her feel good to know that.

It near about killed me.

On the night that group of boys and the rest of the class of 2011 graduated, they honored Matthew. School administrators mentioned his name. A collage of pictures sat on an easel near the stage. Richard and Mary Anne were there to see the boys we shared with them finish their high school days and begin the next chapter without Matthew. He would not be among the crowd that would gather at my house later that night, to share junk food and Sundrop and each write their names on the kitchen wall I painted with chalkboard paint.

When Walker got up the next day, the next afternoon, he came down the stairs with a rose in his hand, the one they handed to him when he crossed the stage and received his diploma. He went to the drawer where we stored his left over announcements and pulled one from the cardboard box. He said he needed the car. He said he'd be back real soon.

He was going to Matthew.

Walker left his graduation rose, and the linen declaration that they were graduates, on the grave of Matthew Shoener, the little boy whose soccer team beat his own, who loved bugs and dinosaurs and racecar drivers and Jesus, the friend he carried to that place and had to leave behind.

I have written so many times that Walker has the best heart of anyone I know. The heart and the soul get all mixed up in the lines of poets and songwriters. I suppose I did it, too. Though Walker's soul is just fine, thank you, doctors at a big, shiny hospital in a big, shiny city have tried twice now to make his heart beat the way it is supposed to.

They'll have to try again.

Two good men, a cowboy, and a road dog, came to sit with me while I waited long hours for the news we hoped would be good. Margaret Connor, named for her aunt, tried the patience of her parents until they brought her to Charlotte and finally the hospital where she fought to hold back the tears when she learned the docs hadn't done what we came for them to do. My cell phone dinged constantly with text messages of love and support. Facebook was kept alight with concerned posts and encouragement.

Among those fine people holding me up was Mary Anne Shoener.

Walker is on the sofa with a pizza sent to him by my friend and literary agent. He will watch the Tar Heels play and knock wood for every superstitious reason you can imagine. He will worry every tick of the clock if they lead by six hundred points or stay within two.

But he will be here in the morning.

This heart thing is no fun at all. We could take an easier route, put in a pacemaker and most of the worrying would be over, but Walker wants to play ball. So, we keep trying, keep sticking needles in his veins and wires in his arteries so that a boy, really now a young man with a nearly perfect soul can have a heart to match, a heart that allows him to shoot from the free throw line, to slap an opponent's shot away in rejection to the roar of the crowd or his own sense of triumph. We talk about wanting him to live his passion. Some even say it's not fair, not right that a boy so good should have to go through this. Mary Anne said she knew how hard this must be for me.

She also knows how hard it isn't. Mary Anne, my good friend, I know that, too.

ROOM FOR WAITING

It's me and forty-nine old people.

They're waiting on their husbands or wives. I am waiting on a kid not yet twenty.

Nobody can hear so everybody yells. The woman across from me is concerned that she forgot her husband's blood pressure medicine. Her sister is with her but not listening, which means she has a profound loss of hearing. She is reading *Southern Living* magazine and occasionally commenting on a recipe or picture. She doesn't much care for a sofa or a caramel sauce, nor does she think the camellias are going to be as pretty in her yard as they are in the magazine. The man two chairs down just sits with his hands in his lap, repositioning a wadded up Kleenex, unfolding it and folding it, crunching it and smoothing it out. I smiled at him and it made him cry.

For those who need introducing, this is Amy. The four of you are the ones I chose to write to. Amy takes pictures. She calls them images so I try to as well. Amy and I met when we were trapped with a one woman freak show at a literary conference, a woman who fancies herself a fine

Christian woman who, later, stole a story of mine and tried to make Amy sound flighty and shallow in a piece she wrote that never saw the light of day.

She thought we were loose women, which we are but that is beside the point.

I introduce all y'all because you have to be family now. I require it.

Say hey to Amy, y'all. Amy, say hey to your new family.

The four of you are the folks I am thinking of on this fucked up day. You are the ones I miss. You are the ones who make me smile when I think of something you said or did.

There's a woman with a brocade jacket, enough gold to pay down the national debt, and an expensive bag, but she's wearing pristine white tennis shoes and ankle socks. Her hair would not move in a Texas tornado. She is fond of making faces that indicate her displeasure with the cheating woman being taken down a notch or two by Dr. Phil on the television y'all can probably hear from where you are. I thought about calling one of y'all and talking dirty just to piss her off but it would upset the man with the wadded up Kleenex. I thought about saying I liked her shoes because she wouldn't know I was making fun of her but I decided I needed Karma to be a bit more on my side today, so I just smiled at that man again. He didn't cry this time.

He asked me if I wanted a butterscotch.

There is another woman. She guarantees everything she says. "He'll be mad when he finds out they ain't gonna let him wear his own pajamas. I can guarantee that." So far, she has guaranteed that President Obama will not be reelected, that they won't have decent soup in the cafeteria, no way, that her little dog will tear something up if she doesn't get home by two o'clock, and that the hem her daughter put in her granddaughter's prom dress ain't gonna hold.

A man closer to my age came in and sat down with his momma. He tried not to smile at the guarantee of a new president but saw me and grinned anyway. He can't stay, he says. He has a case in twenty-five minutes. Lawyer, I reckon. His momma said it was all right but we all can tell it ain't.

The helmet haired woman with the brocade jacket and ankle socks gave him the same disapproving look she did the Dr. Phil slut. She puts me in mind of the time when Amy and I laughed so hard we had to lean hard against Joe Formichella to keep from fallin' in the floor when, at a literary conference, a writer said that if women were offended by what she wrote they were "badly in need of a 'feet to Jesus' orgasm."

Remember that, Amy?

That's the news from the waiting room of the Sanger Heart Institute of Carolina Medical Center. They called. Chris remembers those calls from the last time. They call and say nothing. They think it helps, I suppose. It doesn't. They say stupid shit like, "we're still in the heart" as if I need to be reminded that they are sticking wires in and out of my child. I know that it has taken too long for it to have been as successful as they hoped. Until they let me have him back, I'm here, with the hearing impaired and the judgmental and the sad man who only wants to know that his wife will come home and fix him a grilled cheese while he watches *Wheel of Fortune*.

I love y'all. All y'all. Each of y'all.

HANK AND TENNESSEE

He had called Kemp Sigmon with the good news that his lawyer had fixed things so that he could go to the first home game of the season. Bunker Hill vs. North Lincoln tomorrow night.

They shared a BLT last Monday, Kemp and Greg. The 'why' of it still tears a little at Kemp but for some reason they started reminiscing, talking over old times: Kemp taking Greg to the club level of the Ritz Carlton where Greg was center stage; Kemp taking his boys, his daddy, and Greg to Major League games in big cities far from the limits of Claremont; and their all-time favorite story, the four day drunk Greg spent in Kemp Sigmon's barn.

Greg had gotten himself kicked out of the house, *again*. Kemp, and the rest of us for that matter, saw every moment he spent away from there, away from her, as a little slice of happiness for our friend. Greg had gathered all of his clothes and stuffed them in garbage bags, tossing them one by one in Kemp's barn, using them to make a bed.

In a different story with different characters, Kemp might have suggested sobering up and thinking straight, but it was Greg and it was her, and Kemp said, "Greg, you might should stay liquored up for awhile," and toted him food for the next couple of days.

It was the fall of the year and nut trees were dropping their fruit. Dead drunk, sleeping on bags of his own clothes, Greg thought it sounded like dynamite each time one of them hit the metal roof of the barn.

Kemp came to see his friend, bringing him a sandwich on the third day. Greg, looking to a sky he couldn't see said, "I'm gonna write a damn book someday, Kemp, and the title will be *When the Walnut Hits the Tin*."

I would have trusted him with my life—me and about every woman in this town. If we were within earshot of Greg Isaac, we were safe. The same could not be said for any dumbass whose look was just a little off. Yesterday when the word got out, Karen Harwell was crying to me on the phone. Terri Miller was crying on Facebook along with Lysa and Shelly and Nancy and Rocky and Lori. Reading the messages crippled me for a while until I started thinking.

Greg Isaac had the prettiest women in town crying over him.

This is a summer of loss for Claremont. Just weeks ago we buried Russell Boggs and now we will gather again to say goodbye to Greg Isaac. Folks who don't know any better would think those two men had nothing in common, a preacher and a man who found his salvation in a bottle. Those folks aren't from Claremont.

Bob McDill wrote a song in Nashville and Don Williams sang it. That Yankee writer, Joe Klein, used it in a book he took too long to claim, but that doesn't taint it, doesn't keep it from saying what so many outside the Mason-Dixon miss about this South.

"When I was in school I ran with a kid down the street,
And I watched him burn himself up on bourbon and speed,
But I was smarter than most, and I could choose.
Learned to talk like the man on the six o'clock news.
When I was eighteen, lord, I hit the road
But it really doesn't matter how far I go.
I can still hear the soft southern winds in the live oak trees
And Those Williams Boys they still mean a lot to me,
Hank and Tennessee.
I guess we're all gonna be what we're gonna be,
So what do you do with good ol' boys like me?"

Edie Connor worried aloud to me that we had failed Greg, that as a community, we hadn't done all we could for him. It speaks well of Edie that she worried so over it, but she's wrong and I told her so.

In another place, in another town, Greg would have been somebody's punch line, a man with whom to avoid eye contact, a hurried escape to walk on the other side of the street. In another place, nobody would have posted his bail or given him one more chance to show up for work, and I am damn sure that women who look like Karen Harwell would not have been calling him and leaving messages of love and concern. In another town, the most successful of businessmen would not have burned up their cell phones planning whatever was needed to see that our goodbye to Greg was done properly. In another town, the bar owner who had to turn him away more than once would not ask if he needed to reach for his checkbook to bury the man.

But, this is not another place.

Here in Claremont we know that it takes both Hank and Tennessee to make a culture, to shape a world, that both the gentle and the angry come together to give us someone to pray to and someone to pray about. Russell would be the first to say his loss to us is no greater than Greg's.

I will be the second.

I misjudged this one. I thought we had more time, more days at The Café to sit and talk, more time to listen to the secrets Greg Isaac knew and wanted to tell me. I wasn't paying good attention to how scarce his shelter had become, how hard the rain was pounding. But, I believe it was time. I believe he was tired.

I believe he was spent.

THE OLD FAMILIAR PLACES

delivered July 28, 2010, at the funeral of Rev. Col. James Russell Boggs, Claremont, North Carolina, St. Marks Lutheran Church

Russell Boggs and I agreed on everything.

He was an impeccably well-dressed military man, a colonel, a preacher who wrote formal notes for every occasion and spoke with perfect diction.

I am a half-hippie, half-cowgirl backslider who cusses more than she should and wears jeans to a funeral.

But we agreed on everything.

We were of the same mind on every social and political issue facing our country, every election, every candidate. More importantly and far more critical to our continued peace and prosperity, Russell and I were in full agreement on who should receive Claremont Yard of the Month. If I voiced an opinion, I could count on Russell being my own one man "Amen" chorus. Russell and I agreed on everything except what color the napkins should be at one of our Dinners with the Author, and to this day, I know that I was right.

My obvious superiority in the decorating arts became clear the day Russell Boggs and I considered strangling one another in his front yard.

The Christmas before, Russell had told me a lovely story that he and Mary were once stationed in Williamsburg and promised themselves that one year they would decorate their home in live greenery and fruit. They talked about it every year but, he said, "We are too old now so I suppose that will never be."

Donna Buchanan and I supposed differently.

When I told Russell the very next Christmas that Donna and I had organized folks in town to help us decorate their home in traditional Williamsburg Christmas trimming, he invited me to come to the house for tea. He and Mary wanted to thank me properly.

That was a lie. It was a trick and I fell for it. The invitation was little more than a ruse to get me over there so he could give me three books on Christmas in Williamsburg. He had several pages marked. He went to Barnes and Noble later that week and bought a fourth book, just in case the notes he had made on the other three were unclear to me.

Donna and I worked for several nights sticking greenery in floral foam, pulling wire through apples and oranges and twisting them in and out of branches cut from Russell's Leyland cypress trees. He checked on our progress several times. Donna and I thought it was funny.

Until it wasn't.

On the day we hung the heavy garland around the arched doorway and stuck the pineapple in the perfectly measured center at the top, a job for which we had to use two ladders and a makeshift pulley system, we stood back to admire our efforts.

Russell said, "Dear, don't you think we should have two oranges and an apple grouped together on the right, the same way they are on the left."

I said I did not. I did not think that at all. "It was my intention, Russell, for it to be asymmetrical. It's more appealing that way."

He said, "That's marvelous, dear, but do you see what I'm saying?"

I said I did see what he was saying but didn't care all that much. He laughed like he thought it was funny, but he didn't. I told him it was too matchy matchy, too military to have them directly across from one another and Russell said, "Well, I was a colonel, you know."

I told him if he had been that all fired good at it, he would have been a general.

"Perhaps you're not understanding me," he said.

I replied, "Russell, I am both understanding you and disagreeing with you. I am doing both those things at the same time."

Russell said, "Oh, you are so funny. Maybe we could put two apples and ONE orange across from the other grouping." I considered kicking him really hard and runnin'.

Instead, I told him I was going inside to say hello to Mary, and Russell thought that was a fine idea.

In my heavy coat and stocking hat, I slumped in a chair next to Mary. She was wrapping note cards with ribbon to put in a basket by the door so they would have gifts for people who dropped by unexpectedly. She asked how it was going outside.

"Mary," I said, "Russell is bossy."

She dropped her ribbon and laughed. Mary put her hands in her lap, the way I have seen her do so many times, the way a lady sits when addressing a serious situation.

"You know," she said, "you and Russell are just alike. You and Russell are do-ers. You think of something and you do it. Me, I have the best of intentions but I don't follow through. For example, I saw you through the window and thought, I should go say hello to Shari, but I didn't."

She went on.

"So many times, Russell and I will be coming back from a meeting at church or maybe the Lion's Club and Russell will be so angry. He will be going on and on about someone and say, 'Oh, that, whoever, just HAS to have his way about everything. He never thinks anyone else is right.' And I will just look out the car window and smile. You see, Russell doesn't know he is that way."

I went outside, climbed the ladder and wired up two oranges and an apple. We made the front page of the Newton paper.

In the weeks after Russell and Mary left Claremont, I grieved so hard I came to believe I would never get over it, losing them, losing him. The Christmas after they left, I took a walk very late one night. I stood in front of their house, hating it, hating the sight of it. I thought about throwing rocks at it and figured the police chief would understand. Instead, I just stopped going anywhere near that hateful house, that house that just let them walk out and get gone, gone from us.

There's a long list of things Russell did for this town. That's for the preacher to talk about. Russell liked lists. They appealed to his sense of order and accomplishment and his grand sense of ceremony. But he wanted me to speak, asked me to do this a long time ago and he had to know what I would say would not be of lists and honors and awards. I believe he wanted me to talk about neighbors.

In *To Kill A Mockingbird*, Harper Lee wrote, "Neighbors bring food with death, flowers with sickness, and little things in between."

Russell was our neighbor. There's only a thousand of us in two and a half square miles so all of us can claim him. He brought us flowers and food, but it is the little things in between that mean the most.

Judy Setzer has a letter he wrote to her after he saw her putting flowers on a grave. Gaye Morrison has his childhood rocking horse. Linda Hewitt wanted something that belonged to him so badly that she went to his yard sale and bought the ugliest lamp you have ever seen in your life. I have an old wardrobe, a painting of a farm, and a duck decoy. We keep these things, these pieces of Russell, the letters, the art, the hideous lamp, to hold on to some part of him.

And I know why.

Russell and I, known to be big time Democrats, which can get a person shunned in this county, always wondered why our party flat loves to use the word "tolerance." You'll hear it in just about every speech given on the left side of the aisle. It's a bad word, a horrible word. Russell Boggs was not tolerant. In fact, he was highly intolerant. He did not tolerate any of us.

He accepted all of us, every one of us. You knew it, felt it within minutes of meeting him. There are people who live their whole lives and never know what that is like, complete acceptance. We know it. We know it because we knew Russell. Margaret Garrison told me that she does not feel sorry for any of us, not for any of us who are crying and sad today. She feels sorry for the people who don't know that there is a reason to be sad and grieving, for that means they did not know Russell Boggs. On this day, it is the sad and the grieving who are lucky.

We have known acceptance.

He knew of no division among people because of differences of color or bank balance. He believed that people living in a small town in rural North Carolina deserved musicals and writers and art and he worked to bring them all to us. He told me, 152 times, that he had secured the number one German band in the Southeast for that first Oktoberfest and he completely ignored me when I said, "Really, Russell, Number ONE? How many German bands are there in the Southeast. I mean, it ain't like we're eat up with 'em, right?"

Those boys showed up, drank beer out behind the church between sets, and would you believe they played Dixie at the end of the night? As far as I'm concerned, they are the number one German band in the Southeast.

We, the sad and the grieving, have known acceptance, the arts, and we have seen true love. We know that it exists. We saw it every day between Russell and his bride.

The year we decorated the house for them, Russell and Mary invited the town for an open house on Christmas Eve. Mary told us the story of their courtship, that she had been engaged to another when Russell came calling with flowers picked from his mother's garden. She gave back the ring and said to a room full of people sitting around her Christmas tree, "I have been in love with him every day since."

What always struck me was their courtesy to one another. They always said, "please" and "thank you" and Mary would say, "Excuse me, Russell, for interrupting." Not me. I will stop a total stranger in line at the grocery and tell him he is not telling a story correctly. All those years, all those days in company with one another, and they still used courtesy. I used to find excuses to go to their house so I could listen to them talk to each other, not to me. I wanted to be there, just to watch, just to listen.

I tend not to always remember what I have seen but can remember, nearly verbatim, what I have heard. It helps to have that going for me when I write. Russell would have people in for dinner and ask me to mimic Margaret Garrison, which by the way I do very well. It was my party trick. If I tried really, really hard, I could mimic Mary and he loved it. Said I sounded just like her. My impersonation of Russell, however, left him a little cold. He said I made him sound fussy. It wasn't hard to imitate him. It still isn't. All you have to do is use the word, "marvelous." It was his favorite. He used it four times in the last letter he wrote to me.

The book by the author coming to town was "just marvelous," the program he watched on PBS was "simply marvelous," the number one German band in the Southeast was going to be "marvelous." He meant it each time he said it.

I would give almost anything to hear him say it just one more time.

With apologies to all the preachers in the room and to all those who feel better believing that Russell is in heaven, in a better place, I have to tell you … I don't believe he is there. I don't believe he would go without Mary. Whatever your vision is of heaven, it would be nothing to Russell if Mary isn't there. I think he comes and goes as he pleases. I believe that Russell earned that right. I would bet my last dollar that St. Peter gave him a key.

Besides, I have seen him, haven't you? I have seen Russell this past week in all the old familiar places. I saw him on Sunday morning, walking a step behind Glenn Morrison on his way home from church. The mayor was whistling, like he always does, and didn't see that Russell was with him. But I did. Just a while ago, he had his arm around Katie Carpenter. And earlier today he was in line at The Café, wearing his tweed driving cap, ordering sandwiches to take back to Mary. He looked up, right at me. I am sure of it. He will be at the next Lions Club meeting, sitting next to Nancy Murray. He will wear a plaid shirt, neatly pressed.

I don't want to throw rocks at that house anymore. It is a comfort to me. I saw him there. I will always see him there, in the garden, wearing that silly pith helmet. He will raise his hand to wave to me, just a little, but he will not speak.

He doesn't have to.

For the rest of my time, if I am gone tomorrow or live for a thousand years, I'll Be Seeing You, Russell, in all those old familiar places.

"I'll find you in the morning sun, and when the night is new,
I'll be looking at the moon.
But, I'll be seeing you."

THE HAND THAT ROCKS THE CRADLE

Walker was sweeping cobwebs from places I could not reach while Taylor Simmons bounced a basketball in the barn. Walker yelled, "Hey, Mom, somebody is here—in a car—somebody I don't—oh wait..." Stepping into the feed room, he said, "Mom, come on. It's Russell Boggs' son."

Terry had brought his mother home.

Mary Boggs sent the letter last week. She would be in Claremont for the Cloninger reunion and would like to see me. It was not a request. It is her second letter to me since Russell died. I recognized her handwriting before I had pulled it from the mailbox. With Mary's perfect manners and sense of grace, I knew it would be a thank you note, the proper handwritten acknowledgement that I had honored Russell's request and spoken at his funeral, a service she was too ill to attend. My great fear was that I had disappointed her.

She wrote that she often thought of the old song, *"I'll Never Smile Again Until I Smile With You,"* in the days after what she called "Russell's departure," unable to refer to death and her husband in the same sentence.

But, she wrote, when they played an audiotape of the service for her, while I was talking she "laughed out loud."

Russell must have liked that.

Russell was a talker. Mary is not. That is not to say that she hasn't used her quiet Southern whisper to make a point or take a stand. When they were at a church in Montgomery, just down the street from where Dr. King preached, Mary got on a city bus and took a seat. She took a seat in the back.

She would not be moved.

When a brick was thrown through her living room window, a reminder that proper white Southern preachers and their wives were not to march in the street, not to stand, their pale hands locked together with hands of color, Mary kept walking. And, upon their return to Claremont, at a formal dinner party hosted by the dean of Lenior Rhyne College, they were asked why, of all the places they had lived, of all the countries they had called home, why they would choose to return to Claremont, North Carolina. Russell, ready to answer the question, heard Mary speak. To a table of hushed dinner guests, Mary politely answered,

"So we could *personally* vote against Senator Helms."

Mary told me once of remembering the first election of President Roosevelt. Her mother had been widowed a few months before, but Mary remembered that they walked across town, hand in hand, to the home of friends who owned a radio. Mary was eight years old. She said she could still hear the crackle of the on-the-air voice reporting election results. It was important to her mother that she be listening when Franklin Delano Roosevelt became her president.

She said it just like that, "her president."

I remember watching the Watergate hearings. I was twelve. Maybe then, the die was cast: fat men with Southern accents are good, fat men with flat top haircuts and homogenized speech are bad, bad men. I thought Senator Sam must be a fine grandfather. He seemed so much wiser than the men he was in charge of questioning and all the best men I knew wore short sleeve white shirts and black ties.

It *was* summertime.

Abbie was twenty-seven when she stood in line for hours waiting to get into a Hillary Clinton rally. When she was close enough to the door she called her right wing conservative Christian father and stepmother and they hurriedly brought Matilda to her. They dressed her in tiny jeans and a onesie that read "Hillary Cares About Me," and got Matilda in her mother's arms in time to be able to say, one day, that she was there when the first woman to have a serious shot at the Oval Office spoke in her home state. Later, Abbie worked her way to the Senator, who took one look at Matilda and said, "And who is *this*?" Holding her, Hillary Clinton posed for a picture with my baby and my baby's baby. A secret service agent nodded toward Matilda and asked Abbie, "How old?" and Abbie answered, "Nine months." The picture sits in a frame on my desk. Matilda is sucking her thumb, Abbie is beaming, and the woman who would soon be Secretary of State looks more like a momma who loves babies than a politician.

At Greg Isaac's funeral, Tony Garrison leaned across Margaret and said to me, "Listen, when I die, if Glenn Beck can't make it to Claremont in time, will you speak at my funeral?"

He thinks he's hilarious. If I call for Margaret and Tony answers the phone, he often yells, "Margaret, it's Hillary!" When their grandson was four years old, I taught him to say, "Grandpa Tony is a Nazi." Grandpa Tony taught him to say, "Miss Shari is a Communist." Tony repeatedly asked me if while I was at it, getting authors to come to town, maybe I could get Bill O'Reilly to come. "He's got a couple of books out, you know." I told him that I would absolutely love to invite Bill to town...as soon as I figure out exactly where to bury the body.

I love Tony Garrison and he loves me. He told me so once when I was sobbing because Russell and Mary were moving to Texas, and like Margaret says, he "can't take it back, now." I love Edie Connor and nobody thinks I am further left of the political spectrum than Miss Edie. Her oldest calls me his "liberal momma." But, I triple-dog-dare you to find a Democrat, any Democrat, who does more volunteer work, more anonymous giving, more dropping by with food for the sick and blankets for new babies than Edie...and, Alisa Carpenter tries not to think about what I'm up to on Election Day.

When Mary got out of the car this afternoon I tried to remember if I have ever seen her without Russell. I don't believe I have. She looked good and I told her so. She thanked me and said that was a much nicer thing to say than two women she talked to earlier who told her she had gained weight, weight much needed and even now can't add up to a

103

hundred pounds. I whispered, "Were they Yankees, Mary? Southern women would never say that, would they?"

She laughed at that.

Walker came from the barn to see her. Taylor introduced himself like the fine and well-raised boy that he is.

"Pleased to meet you," she said. "I'm Mary Boggs."

Taylor got his driver's license this week. He thought it was funny to post on my Facebook wall that the best part of that particular milestone was getting to preregister to vote. He wanted to make sure I understood that he had signed up for the *Right* party."

His mother swears she doesn't know where his political views came from, but she said she was just proud that he had them.

Me, too.

I told Taylor in a long discussion about being politically active that he should never let apathy or a difference of opinion keep him from working on a campaign or choosing a career as a political operative. I told him that the only thing I hated was not caring.

We have to care.

I like the saying, "The hand that rocks the cradle rules the world." It makes sense and gives credit, and blame I suppose, to parents for what our kids see and hear from us. Did Abbie become politically active because of my interest? Maybe. Most likely she formed her own opinions and found her own way. She always does. Will Matilda look at a picture of the baby version of herself being held by a woman she will not remember and feel she needs to march in the streets for a cause she believes in? If so, do yourself a favor and get out of her way. Matilda has several generations of strong-willed women on all branches of her family tree.

She might should come with a warning label.

Today Terry Boggs told me a story I don't believe I'd heard. He said he asked his father once why he had such a strong sense of justice, of political activism. Terry said to Russell that he knew it couldn't just be his Sunday School lessons. He wanted to know where it started, the life of service and community involvement his parents had led and taught to him.

Russell told him that in his high school years the rural electric co-op had come to Claremont to hook up. They would have lights to read by and heat in rooms that had been without. Russell's family was to be first on the list.

Sharecroppers, black families, lived on parts of the Boggs land, and Russell's father, thrilled with the thought of cooling fans in hot Southern summers, asked the coop if they would be connecting to all the homes on his land on the same day or if it would take more time than that. He was told that his home was the only one to be receiving electrical power.

The father of the man who would become the moral compass for this town told the co-op that their power would not be welcome until it came to all of them, to "all of us," he said. Instead of being first, the Boggs family was last. Their house came immediately after the homes of the sharecroppers.

And so it began.

If Taylor runs for the senate someday, I will, most likely, vote for him. He is a smart kid with a good heart. And I know his momma and that trumps any political platform. If he does, if he runs, I hope he remembers today. I hope he remembers the handshake.

"Pleased to meet you. I'm Mary Boggs."

CAROLINA GIRL

I had all I could take.

The fine folks at The Weather Channel decided to dedicate nearly all their coverage to what a hurricane named Irene would do north of the Mason-Dixon. The fact that she is headed straight for Cape Hatteras is evidently less of a story than shutting down the subway in The Big Apple.

Not to me.

This late in the evening, I find myself waiting on the decisions this hurricane will make, remembering part of a book by a sexy Frenchman named Guy who wrote about the futility in trying to impress Mother Nature, and thinking how the bigger mistake was made when they named this thing. Everybody knows not to piss off anyone named Irene.

But mostly I have surprised myself in how deeply wounded I was at the lack of televised concern for the coast of my state. To be honest, I have always felt a little, well, competitive with the beach, a place so intoxicating that the Hokes would shut down the Claremont Café for an entire week just to be there, an allure so strong that four and five families would pool their money to share a two bedroom condo just to get sand in their shorts and make their own bologna sandwiches.

I am a mountain girl.

For reasons I cannot explain, I know where I am when I am in the mountains. I can't navigate Hickory to save my own ass, but I can be at nearly any crossroad in the Blue Ridge and know which way to turn to get to Linville Gorge.

I love Linville.

I can feel Grandfather Mountain breathing, have been sure he winked at me, certain I have heard angels sigh just to be near him. I have fought back fear to stand on his chin and let the ashes of a good dog fly into the wind, watched the ravens soar and dip, unable to tell if they were fighting that same wind or enjoying it, using it to hold them up in what is clearly heaven. I know the lines to bluegrass music born in those hills, those hollers, and once saw two bobcat kittens cross the Parkway in front of me and waited on the hill so that I could stop the station wagon with New Jersey tags behind me and point, allowing the momma and the children buckled in the back to see them there. The daddy driving resisted the urge to honk but drummed his thumbs on the steering wheel.

I did not care. His young'uns saw two baby bobcats in the Carolina mountains.

I have said to everyone that if the Million Dollar Prize Patrol took a notion to show up at my door I would buy a place in the mountains, not the beach. Never the beach. But I learned today that I can be pretty damn territorial about the coastline of my home state, too. It's a good thing to learn.

Coastal folks speak a language I don't understand. It is a language of sailors and fishermen. I know none of that. They talk of what color flag is flying and high and low tides, of "the catch," the haul, the day spent on a vessel that sways and bobs in blue that goes on forever, farther than anyone can see even sitting on their daddy's shoulders, and that is a long damn way. I don't know how to tie proper knots or hoist or lower a sheet of canvas to get a boat to go right or left. I don't know how to open a lobster trap. I can barely open a lobster.

I do know to dip his ass in butter, but that doesn't count for all that much.

I wrapped myself in a blanket one afternoon to sit on the shore of Mobile Bay and listen to Jimbo Meador talk about it, the water, the bay—his bay. I do believe that when no one is watching, Jimbo can breathe underwater, but when I asked him if that was true he denied it. That water belongs to Jimbo and to Alabama. It ain't mine though lord it was a blessed afternoon listening to him tell me of it, describe a Jubilee and a gull net. Mentioning the Outer Banks to him brought a story from him of reading Ruark's, *The Old Man and the Boy*, how he followed along to every place written about on those pages that made readers out of men who swore they cared nothing for book stories. Jimbo told me that there was no place like the Outer Banks. I felt proud they belonged to Carolina and a little sorry for a man who often slips out of whatever he is wearing just to get wet, to swim in the brackish water outside a house that belonged to his wife's family before he bought it for her.

Least, that's how he tells it.

In my own time on the Outer Banks, I have stood before the great lighthouses and daydreamed a little about living in one, of climbing the stairs to strike a match and in that simple act avert disaster and bring a daddy home to his family. I listened as the story of Whalehead Club was told to me, the rich man so offended at the "Men Only" policies of the Yacht Club, so incensed that his wife could not join him for dinner and a cigar, that he built his own, a piece of architectural art on Corolla. I've seen the mustangs pick through the beach grasses for sea oats, their winter coats long and thick, and hoped they would never know the feel of a saddle on their backs, a bit in their mouths. I've stood on the same shore where the pirates walked in circles, lanterns tied around the necks of the horses they led, mimicking a lighthouse and causing ships to run aground in the best spot to be robbed.

They call it Nags Head on account of that history. Something stirred when I read *Our State Magazine's* story on the cowboy who looks after those horses. That writer shined a soft light on folks mostly overlooked, defining them with poetry and treating them with dignity. I respect that more than any Pulitzer they hand out. I walked the edge of Pamlico Sound and added so many species of ducks and water birds to my Life List, I got writer's cramp.

Though I know several facts and legends about the coastline of North Carolina, I do not know it. I haven't thought of it as mine. It hasn't belonged to me nor I to it the way I am connected to the mountains.

I know what I know. I know what I don't.

I know that here, in these foothills, it is safe and in your best interest to take a swig of moonshine if it is handed to you by Tim Yount, and a mistake of biblical portion to take one from Gary Sigmon. The first will go down smooth and taste like the fall air smells. The second might could cause you not to come to for several days. I know that it was like playing with fire if Miss Janie had to yell your order more than twice at The Café, and that she decided on her own whim how much it would cost, ignoring any menu or what you paid for that same sandwich the day before. I know that if Willie Hewitt tells you that you almost look good enough to throw the make on, it is a compliment and that it won't bother his wife one little bit.

I know that if Miss Maebelle comes through the door, Miss Glenna will follow. I know that nobody bakes pound cake like Miss Peggy, and that if I cough while walking down the street or just ain't lookin' like I feel good, fourteen women will show up at my house with chicken pie or potato salad. I know that the churches stagger their Christmas Eve services so folks can make it to each one if they give it any kind of good try.

Today, as I defended the honor of our coastline, I learned that I am connected to it. I am bound to that string of land, some of it no wider than a football field, by Bev who has fought cancer like a pissed off badger and uses the same set of claws and teeth to go after chemical dumps and corporate giants that find loopholes. I am tied to that unique and strange combination of earth and sky and water by Miss Blue. She was my first fan, the first one that wasn't crazy. She wrote a letter to a magazine that published my story, and then wrote nice things to me. I think about her often but forget to write. I am ashamed of that. I should know better. It got so I would send stories to Blue before the editors saw them. She's never criticized a word.

I am tethered to the coastal city of Wilmington by Nicki Leone, today called a goddess because of her constant support of writers and their books, her work to promote and protect the independent bookstores of the South, and her unmatched generosity in including me in a list of recommended reading that made its way to Nashville and onto the radio.

I know these women.

I stopped for breakfast on Hatteras and ordered scrambled eggs and toast. There was a fisherman sitting at the bar. He was drinking a Budweiser at eight in the morning.

I know one more thing. He's my people.

By biology, I am a half-breed. The maternal side is Midwestern. They never did understand or like me all that much. By virtue of my daddy, I am Southern, I am Tennessee, so much working hill people that they said, "you'uns," not "y'all." Not even "all y'all."

That is the side that took.

But I am Carolina by choice, my choice, all of Carolina. I get to claim it all. It's mine by the hand done stitching of friends, and laughter, and tears. I am a Carolina Girl because I choose to be.

I am Claremont by the grace of all that is holy.

HOME BY NOW

I've never been in love with my house.

It was a marriage of convenience. I needed a place to live and it needed someone to pay the heat bill. It lacked anything that would stir passion in me, but I believed I could fake it for what it did have. I've never seen stars or heard violins while walking through it.

Walker loved it from the beginning. He always felt our other home lacked privacy, sitting on a corner, both doors visible from two streets. He heard wild turkeys in the woods on the first night in this house and was home. He fell hard. He's always seen the good. Nate and Abbie walked through it before the closing and thought it was great. Abbie was right when she said, "It has a perfect layout, Mom." She's always been one to see the practical. She and Nate thought of building one just like it.

I went through the motions.

I spent good money on renovating the barn. It was a love at first sight that only grew stronger. I am at peace within its walls, made whole by every minute spent caring for it. While hiding from a tornado in the hallway bathroom of the house, with a retriever I love and a dachshund I don't even like all that much, my consuming fear was not for the roof above me or the old oaks and pecan trees. I whispered to wind that skipped us all together, "Don't take my barn."

I finally, after two years, painted my room. It helped. I tore out a wall in the kitchen. Now that did make things more interesting, but not for long. The best thing about that decision was it gave me a wider view of the barn while chopping onions or scrambling eggs. It was still just a house.

It's been nearly three years. If I could multiply—hell, if I could add, I'd know how many days that is. There have been, only now and then, loving moments in a loveless union. I've thought of leaving it a hundred times, of walking out the back door without bothering to lock it, of finding the true love I believe is out there somewhere, even if its plaster is long past smooth and its paint is peeling. I never do.

I stay. I keep working on it.

I stopped mourning the house that died a while back, stopped feeling the loss. It has become a story I tell, not a pain I feel. What I continued to want were my neighbors. I wanted P.J. and Brenda, Nick and Jan and Donna. Mostly, I wanted Miss Jean.

What I got was Tim Yount.

Tim wasn't really even my neighbor at first. Until he got free of a woman who did not deserve him, Tim used that great old house across the road from mine only as an office defying a city zoning ordinance nobody much cared about anyway. I used to see him in The Café, reading the morning paper, sometimes two. I didn't think I cared much for him. I was wrong about that.

Tim has the quick wit. I play host to writers, Pulitzer Prize winners, Bronze Star recipients, folks with big brains and big words. Tim is quicker on the draw than any one of them. He once told me about a car breaking down in California and the mechanic who came to get it running. He heard Tim talk and said, "Where are you from?" Tim was heavy on Southern and light on Malibu. I couldn't help but think, that guy heard an accent and mistakenly assumed all kinds of wrongs. He was talking to a man who could verbally spar with kings and Presidents—and kick their ass.

Tim has a musician friend, Jonathan Birchfield. Tim said I should hear him play sometime. Roxanne Moser bought me his CD. Jonathan brought it by while I had a house full of writers. One of them said, "Who was that?"

"Some Singer-Boy," I answered.

But I listened to his music and it was good. His lyrics were good and the boys playing were good. Mostly, to be a good neighbor to Tim, I called Birchfield up and asked for an interview, tried to find a story to write about a guy who wrote a song about my Claremont Café. We talked of our shared love of Jackson Browne and Larry McMurtry books. He invited me to a benefit concert in Valdese, arranged an All Access Pass. I decided to show up.

This is what I know. All good things come to me by way of Claremont. With the exception of my children, and through one of them, my grandbabies, everything good in my life came to me, or came back to me, because of this town. It's a fact.

Backstage, I found my story in a songwriter who paints pictures with words the way other artists work in oils. We've had lunch at The Café twice since then, Michael Reno Harrell and me. Yesterday, Willie Hewitt came through the door and said, "There's Shari and her hippie friend." Raymond wanted to know if I was goin' out with him. Raymond worries over my single status, believes it is high time I took a husband.

You know you are sorry when the town drunk who lives in a storage unit thinks your ability to attract a man is fast leaving.

I found a story in a cowboy who came through the back door and said, "Hi." Jonathan would tell me he was a guitar god. A dobro player would call him the "best electric guitar player on the East Coast." I would come to appreciate him for a song he sang in my living room when the subjects of my next magazine story all came for a bowl of my chicken and sausage gumbo.

They left their guitar cases scattered around my house like the writers leave their laptops and backpacks. They pulled their chairs in a circle while my dog took her place on the rug and went to sleep.

I wanted Miss Jean. I got Tim. Together we have emptied a jar of moonshine he made in his own kitchen while a fifty dollar bottle of Blanton's bourbon sat on a shelf not five feet from us, and I have laughed harder than I once thought possible. He's been in several of my stories. An English teacher and a literary agent told me that I am at my best when my writing includes something Tim has said. From Tim, I got Jonathan. From Jonathan, I got music. From music, I got a home.

This morning, I woke and pulled on my jeans for the first of many daily trips to my barn, slipping from the one I am supposed to love to the one I do. But today it was different the moment I opened my bedroom door.

I heard it.

Lilly's nails clicked in time on a laminate floor I've openly cussed to the tones of acoustic guitars. From the walls that soaked it in some weeks ago, I heard a cowboy sing.

"Sun is shining through your window
Pretty curtains of lace.
Though I've never been here before
I don't feel out of place.
All my life I've been alone
but, I'm here somehow.
I was thinkin', if I lived here,
I'd be home by now."

It's not my old street where Nick Colson, still in his boxer shorts, would go get the morning paper. It is where Tim leaves clean casserole dishes on the bench outside my back door when I lie to him about cooking too much and fix supper for him and his good boy. It's not where Kevin Isenhour and I pounded the Yard of the Month sign into the front lawn at Miss Jean's house and surprised her with the award. It is where we raised money for a boy who needed it and I took my first but not my last drink of Apple Pie. It's not where Saturday night drunks miss their aim and run into the privet hedge bringing all the neighbors to the corner to speculate as to his blood alcohol level. It is where guitar players show up now and then, and feed a need I have for music as much as most folks need oxygen.

It's still Claremont.

And, I was thinking, since I live here, I should be home by now.

FLIGHT

I took the barstool at the corner, well away from the small gathering of men at the other end.

I came to listen to the woman and her guitar. I ordered a beer and pulled the phone from my pocket to send the word. I wanted him to know where I was.

Just in case.

She sang a song I knew better than she did, about a Captured Angel waiting to make a break. I've known that song since an old friend brought the vinyl album named for it to my house in a place I would fly away from as soon as I could kick the cage door open, and I have been living the lyrics ever since.

I've done some damage. I've hurt men who did not deserve it because they failed to see the tattered edges and missing feathers in my wings, wings that drag the ground collecting the dust of a road I hear call me all too often, a call I tend to answer sooner or later. They either believed they could quiet the call or it did go silent long enough for me to believe it, too, that this one would stick. I would make a list of all the reasons I should stay when wind howled through pines and whispered to a gypsy soul I have come to accept, as those frayed wings began to gather around me, keeping pleas of love or logic from ever reaching any place that could feel it.

It wasn't always my fault. A few of the scars in the soft downy layer, the lining designed to keep out bitter cold and drowning rain, were not of my making. I found rocks to throw myself against either in blindness to their ability to wound me or the belief that I deserved it. But leaving is what I know. No shackles yet have kept me from it once I've made up my mind to take flight. It has saved me, more than once.

It's been awhile now that I've thought, maybe, this was the one. I keep waiting to hear the highway, to feel the feathers pick up a breeze. It doesn't come.

I paid for my beer telling the bartender I would only be having one. No need to run a tab. He came, waiving another bottle at me anyway, said a gentlemen wanted to buy it for me, wondered would I take it. Five stools down, there was a nod when I thanked him. He moved in three closer. He asked if I was from around there and laughed when I said, "Claremont," not knowing that's about as quick a way to piss me off as any there is. He asked me what I did for a living before he ran out of questions and said he liked Tom Clancy but just the movies, not the books. I started to feel sorry for him when he told me he didn't like this bar, this town, or sports because "they're mindless." I told him, in fact, they were not.

I checked my phone again.

A few more questions occurred to him. He asked if I knew a really old song called "Pretty Woman" and I laughed though I really did try not to. He said I was pretty and I thanked him for that. He asked if my writing was "like, a thing?" and I said it was exactly like a thing. He shook his head and said he worked in a factory that made furniture. He hated that, too. He asked me if I knew Thomas Hunter. It took him describing a movie before I realized he was referring to Hunter S. Thompson and told him that, no, I did not know him and even if I did, he was dead by his own hand and I was beginning to understand why. He didn't get that joke.

I checked my phone and smiled thinking of a man who would.

He asked me why I had on cowboy boots, if I "liked horses, or something." I told him I always wear them. He said that they looked like they'd hurt and used the bar for balance to show me his Adidas knockoffs, said he preferred comfort to having his toes squished together in the pointed end of a boot, but he reckoned I'd have a hard time running away in those boots so I'd be easier to catch. His comfortable sneakers did not spare him the pinch when I said I didn't need fast shoes to know how to get gone.

He spoke of his brother, which was my chance. I didn't let it pass. "How old is he?" I asked him. He said he was his age, thirty one, then corrected himself and said he was close to his age. I sent a text. Couldn't help it. The bartender gave me a look and raised his chin, a silent offer to intervene but I shook it off. He didn't know. He couldn't see those wings from where he was standing.

Before he would give up he would ask if I wanted to friend him on Facebook and confess that he had lied about his age, that he was, in truth, twenty-nine, but he guessed I might be in my thirties so he thought he should be, too. There might have been a time when that flattered me. I reckon most women would have been, but I wasn't blessed with that kind of mind. I checked my phone again, sent a message, and reached for my coat.

I learned a long time ago what I don't want. I'm learning what it is I do. I still believe that there is a higher love and I am capable of it, of having it, of earning it. I like taking care of a man. I like the work of it. I tried, for a time, to not like it but with enough road passing under you, you learn to accept things about yourself even as your children or your best friends beg you to change them. I like to cook and watch a man enjoying eating. I like to fold shirts the way he likes to find them in his drawer. I will press a crease in jeans if that is the way he wears them. I will give him a thousand smiles and it will cost him nothing.

And, I will wait for him to notice that there is no crying baby I cannot rock to sleep, no song I have heard more than twice without being able to recite the lyrics. I will wait for him to read the words I write and find the reason I chose them. I will wait for him to believe that music and magic lives in me, that I can see things others miss because of the best thing about me which is that I pay attention.

But I won't wait forever. I will fly. It's what I know. I cannot be captured even though it is often what I wish for. A smart and sexy man once said to me that I was waiting for someone to tell me it's all going to be all right. I told him that it wasn't hard to get someone to tell me that.

It was impossible for me to believe it.

If my wings are smaller these days, they are stronger. I do find that I use them less and less for flight but, still, sometimes for cover. I think less like a captured angel and more like a fallen one, still believing that there is coming a moment when I can say, and mean, take anything you want from me, anything...and I will hear it said back to me.

And the highway will be dark and the winds will be still and the only sound will be breathing with no separation in rhythm or depth and the wings, though there, will be remembered for having brought me to that place where I know it's all right.

It's all right.

MONEY FOR NOTHIN'

I was sitting along the wall, had one of the few available chairs at a benefit to honor a gone drummer I'd never met. Musicians from all over Carolina were playing, one band after the next, to raise money for music education and to honor a friend they couldn't help but love even as he couldn't help but drink.

Chris Clifton pointed to a man standing with his back to us, leaned over and said, "Wait till you hear him sing."

Last December, I was in my own living room with Jonathan Birchfield when he was talking about Chris. He said, "Wait till you hear him play."

More years ago than I care to count, at a literary festival in Fairhope, Alabama, the wife of a writer friend of mine motioned toward a small, quiet woman sitting alone in the back row. She pulled at her sleeves and fussed with the hem of her jacket and squirmed and fidgeted like a three-year-old in a church pew. "That's Suzanne Hudson," I was told. "Wait until you read her."

What are they worth, these people who bring us words and music? Joe Formichella tells a great story about his artist brother who grunted and shouted as he painted. The creations that came from him were so powerful that a canvas wasn't enough. They required sound. Joe's family wanted to get the boy "some help." Joe asked why. "Why change him? The world doesn't need more of *you*. The world needs more of *him*."

And there it is.

Sitting in a vineyard in Napa Valley, I listened to the rental car radio, a lousy excuse for a sound system, play Jackson Browne singing "Fountain of Sorrow." The bass half worked and the reception would come and go, but I wept. I was watching my old friend, a dog trainer named Dean, a man so pretty I've seen women stop in their tracks when he smiled. Jackson sang, "*...and at that moment when my camera happened to find you there was just a trace of sorrow in your eyes*," as I watched Dean put the moves on yet another lovely woman he would probably take to bed before the day was over, only to be lonely in the time it took him to forget her name, which he was bound to do. What should Jackson be paid for that? I don't mean writing the song; recording it. What should I pay Jackson for a moment in my life I will never forget, a split second of complete clarity defined by words he strung together and gave to the world, to me. What do I owe Jackson Browne?

What do I owe Jonathan for singing "Bright Baby Blues" in my kitchen and taking me, even in a room full of people, back over years to that vineyard and that day with Dean where we dug through my cassette tapes and played every album Jackson recorded? What do I owe Chris when he plays "Little Wing" and his notes, much more than the lyrics, tell the story of my own circus mind that runs wild and rides with the wind? Was the price of my two beers and four Diet Cokes enough to pay Chris the first time I heard him play "Little Wing," the first time I stared in wonder and the world around me ceased to exist? Should I have ordered a plate of salmon or is a BLT enough to cover the cost of his band that night, as my vision narrowed from the brick walls and leather booths that lined them to nothing but a man and his guitar, pulling enough thought from me to allow me the freedom to write a piece that would be read by over twelve thousand people. How do I pay him for that?

What about Hudson? We are more family than friends now. What do I owe her for two books I can never quite forget, though I have read thousands? Was the price of the book enough? Taking out the cut of the bookstore and the publisher, Hudson gets about a buck-sixteen. I named a bunch of damn rabbits after characters in one of her novels. Is that enough payback for a story that brought a deep and forever understanding of things too mystical to talk about out loud for fear of losing my place at the Back Table of the Claremont Café?

Them boys can't have that kinda talk now.

We pay doctors to heal our bodies and expect artists to take care of our souls for the price of a CD. We'll make a special trip back to the house to stick flip flops in our purses so we don't mess up our pretty painted toes, and tip the pedicure lady an extra ten if she dries them real good, but she'll talk about our jobs, our hair, our periods while the band plays "Into the Mystic" as if it is nothing more than background noise.

Don't talk to me about your job, your hair, or your period while the band plays "Into the Mystic," especially if Ryan Harris is singing it. It pisses me off. I want my gypsy soul rocked, thank you very much.

I told Michael Reno Harrell I was going to single-handedly change the way musicians and writers are viewed, but that was a lie. I am going to ask for some help with that task. Instead of seeing them as our entertainment, how about if we remember that they are the voice of change. Let's cherish them for being the record keepers of how we felt while the historians record what we did. There is a world of difference between those two things, and if we cannot remember how we felt, if we are not reminded of how we *felt*, we are without souls.

Nobody with good sense wants that.

Chris was gone, off smoking when that singer took the stage. I had almost forgotten what Chris had said. That singer boy stepped up to the microphone as I was fishing in my purse for something, not paying attention. I stopped fishing and looked at the stage. "Damn," I said and heard Jaret Carter laugh. He had taken a chair next to a new friend named Sharon and was watching me to see my reaction when Kurt Benfield began to sing. "Can he sing, Shari?" Jaret grinned. "Can the boy flat sing?"

There isn't enough money in the world. But we ought to try, and if we never get them the money they deserve, let's agree to do a lot better in that old department of respect. Let's show some respect, and let's all say, "Thank you."

I'll go first.

THE QUILTER

He keeps breathing to spend one more day with her.

They spend them together, side by side, in reclining chairs watching old Westerns on RFD-TV except for when it's time to give him a shot or count out the dosage of the more than thirty pills he takes over the course of a day. Walker likes the story of how he tricked her into their first date by betting her on some kind of week's-end-productivity at the plant where he was her supervisor, a stacked deck if ever there was one.

I've always suspected she knew that.

Seems like for the past few days I've been thinking quite a bit about true love. I suppose that's a lie. Like most folks, I think about it all the time but the question of what it is, what it looks like, has been coming up in thought and conversation. A good writer friend said he was struggling with the difference between what "is" and what "ought to be." There it is, the king daddy of the battles we fight behind our own eyes, in our own souls. We are bad to think that if we can get someone to either see our point of view or just do what we say, we can turn what is into what ought to be. It never works that way. Long after we learn that hard, hard lesson, we keep trying to make it so.

Writers of song and story tend to run in a pack. It's six of one and a half dozen of the other in deciding if that makes us safer, or the world safer from us. After Chuck said that, about what is and what ought to be, I got to thinking about how the rest of us wear it, that god-awful distance between the two, and I decided that Chris is the best of us at accepting what is, while I want to know *why* it is. Joe refuses to accept what is and Suzanne hides behind Joe from all of what is. Then she writes it worse than it is and slams it shut between the covers of a book to keep it there, away from her and the rest of us, the ones she loves.

I wonder why that is.

Now that's just funny any way you look at it.

I was watching Chris practice his guitar. He showed me a couple of things, said he could either strike the string this way to get a note or the other way to get something completely different and I wondered if that is why. It's the why of something, but I don't know if it is the why of the chicken or the why of the egg. Like the rest of us, he has an artist's soul. Did he use it to become a guitar player because it gives you only what you give it? Hit a chord dead in the middle and you get one sound but bend it, just so, and you get another. It's all up to you and you can spend your life studying it, and Chris has, and still hasn't discovered every possibility. But no matter what, you can't hit a C and get an A.

That's just the way it is.

Joe rages against what is and has changed enough, or seen enough change, to feed his belief that if he works hard, and far more importantly, if he believes deeply, he shall, by god, overcome. We selfishly love this trait in him and count on him for exactly that even while he throws himself against the rocky shore, we want him to keep swimming. We ought to be beat for that. He listens to me, some. I love him far too much to watch it for long. I step in the line of fire now and then, and hold my hand to his chest and in some miracle of trust and love, he looks me in the eye.

And he stops.

Suzanne, well, she's Suzanne Hudson, writer genius. I have seen Chris hug her so completely that he wrapped around her tiny frame until she was almost swallowed up in his everything-is-bigger-in-Texas embrace. She does her best to disappear. Because he loves her, Joe, the fighter of all evil and injustice, the slayer of what is, keeps it from her, protects her for fear it will swallow her up more than a Chris Clifton hug and the Hudson we know will dissolve. Nobody wants that.

Anyway, the southern literary gods and *Publishers Weekly* critics would have our asses for that tragedy.

Amy looks through a lens and in the blink of a shutter captures what is...but makes it better. Why in the hell we ain't all photographers I cannot tell you. That's the way to be now. That is the way-to-be.

I'm trying to do better at accepting what is. I look to Chris for that. He said he knows it is the difference in our art, him behind a guitar and me with only thin paper between me and the harsh world. While it won't let me hide behind it, that transparent page, it does let in the light and the love when it's there, and so I take the angst and the darkness and wait for the sun to come. Chris has to move the thickness of alder and ash to the side for anything to have a direct shot at his heart. Sometimes, he can't see any good reason for that. Thank you, Jesus, sometimes he does.

As for them other two, long before she came along, he had his first heart attack but she signed up anyway and saw him through a few more. Twice it's been the cancer. There's the dia-beet-teeze, the drug allergies, and the mini stroke; a warning of what was to come but when it did, when it hit and stole one good half of him, she found one more way of letting him be the man he was.

She taught my daddy to quilt.

She cuts and pins. He runs the Singer with his good side. Together, they have made more than forty, given away more than half, and shown them to every person who walks through the door. I'll bet you a hundred dollars, right this minute, my daddy has coaxed the mail carrier inside long enough to show off their latest creation. He always, always says the same thing. "She is so good at choosing the colors, ain't ye, Myrnie?"

That right there is poetry, if you ask me.

Where he used to spend his time restoring antique John Deeres, he now runs thread over calico. In the same way he used to wrap a fishing rod so pretty it was worthy of hanging on the wall, now he sews pieces of paisley together in a log cabin pattern. He ain't a bit useless. It might not be the way it ought to be, but it's mighty fine the way it is.

The only one of us to really get it right is my stepmother, Myrna. She, too, is an artist. She paints and cross-stitches and makes Christmas ornaments and a Thanksgiving turkey that put my son in a coma from the bliss of eating so much of it. She can sew and crochet, and my daddy will wear her out sending her to fetch whatever she made and stacked in the closet so everyone can see.

Myrna has an artist's soul.

Somehow, she has learned to accept what is and fight hard enough to change what she can. She can smell an incompetent doctor a mile off and at five-foot and barely nothin' she isn't scared one little bit of telling them they are fired. She has kept him alive to tell me the stories now published in magazines all over this country, and in doing so has seen to it that Matilda and Jack and whatever little bits of perfection Walker brings into this world will know their great, great, great, and back a generation from all of them.

Dad tells me the stories. Myrna has made certain that he can.

We all love each other, truly. Chuck and Chris and Joe and Suzanne and Amy and me and a hundred other Southern artists. We work to accept each other and are pretty good at it really. We may be trying to change the world, all except Chris who accepts it pretty good, but we figure we'd better let our little bit of half crazy remain as is. We need each other.

Dad and Myrna sit in those chairs, watching tractor pulls and gun-fights, sewing quilts and taking them to the sick, the sicker than them, anyway, and make no attempt to change a thing about each other. Far as I can tell, they never have. It took him a few tries, but my daddy found the love of his life and brought to the rest of us a fine example of true love.

He keeps breathing just to spend one more day with her.

STACKING THE DECK

Truth be told, I have always been a little ashamed of my deck, not of its appearance but that it exists as a deck and not as a porch.

Midwesterners have decks. Southerners have porches. I used to say that a lot when I had a hundred year old porch that wrapped all the way around a house I loved. I was pretty snotty about it. It was a location, the definition for which house was mine, the one with the porch. That, or the one with the bushes on the corner that Saturday night drunks ran into when they misjudged the curve of Catawba Street.

I did not build this deck. It came with the house and was, and is, an impressive addition. It has two tiers, lots of room and functions very much like what HGTV calls an outdoor room. I put out flowers and rocking chairs with coordinating cushions that look real good with the rug I bought at Target for $149.00, and added side tables and a bar. Everyone says it looks just like a picture in *Southern Living* magazine, but *Southern Living* would send their photographer to find a porch.

A little over a year ago, three weeks after I had moved into this house, some Southern writer friends came to town. Joe Formichella and Suzanne

Hudson drove up from Waterhole Branch, Alabama and Doug Crandell and his Nancy from around Atlanta. Bay Woods came from Maryland but being that he was born and raised in South Carolina we don't fuss much over his current choice of location. Joe Galloway was here, too, long ago forgiven for being from Texas.

Galloway was in the middle of war stories, some of them knee slappin' hilarious from sixteen years of reporting in other countries, once babysitting a flatulent dog, some not a bit funny from jungle battlefields littered with American boys, too young to die, too old for their mommas to hide them from the draft. Folks were laughing and crying and begging for more and there might have been just a little whiskey, legal and not, when Galloway got a call on his cell. He looked at the caller ID and flipped open his phone. Leaving the circle to stand against the railing of the deck that embarrassed me, Galloway broke down and teared up.

Four boys were coming home.

Bruce Crandall, "Snake Shit," to those who read the book or saw the movie, a helicopter pilot who flew into hell to bring out the wounded, was telling our Joe that finally, finally, he had won a battle he fought with our own government. Four of his missing were found, four of his own, four who had survived the Ia Drang and lived through what took so many others only to vanish off the face of the earth on a mission to deliver breakfast. It didn't seem possible, their disappearance or their recovery, but they were found and brought home because Snake and the sister of one of them who, according to Joe, went from a mild mannered housewife to a hell-bent radical, never gave up.

Joe told us that "Too Tall," Ed Freeman, the other pilot made famous by words Joe Galloway put on paper, words that made their way to a movie screen, on his death bed told Snake not to quit, to bring them home no matter what.

He did.

I had a connection to their homecoming, a role in the story, because Joe got the call while at my house, sitting on my deck. Formichella said he felt the same way, that being there with Galloway when he got the call was a privilege.

But, writers get to change things when they tell a story. I've been tempted to set that one on a porch, take listeners and readers to a slow motion ceiling fan and a lazy wooden swing with Lady Banks roses climbing a trellis behind Galloway as he took the call he had waited on more than forty years. Being on a porch sounded more like the South, more like Carolina.

This weekend, a year and a month later, the same cast of characters, plus several in supporting roles were gathered in Claremont. With four guest rooms and five guest beds in this house, I still had to put Jim Gilbert on a couch. There was a big ol' pile of Southern writers and editors, and again they spent most of their time drinking on my deck. We did other things, too. Nicole King helped me bathe my horse. Formichella did all the prep work for the paella I cooked while holding court with Walker and two of his high school buddies, telling them of a book he wrote on a coaching legend. There was a game of basketball in the barn, the Writers vs. the Varsity Athletes from Bunker Hill High School that only caused the writers to drink more in an attempt to drown their shame. Monday morning, we attended a ceremony in which Claremont honored our veterans. Galloway laid a wreath, spoke to the audience, skipped the invitation to be at much larger gatherings in more important places and came to us. And afterward, of course, we all went to The Café.

Each night we gathered on the deck and talked. Each morning I got up first and shoveled through the carnage, tossed the scattered bottles in the recycling bin and threw away the crumpled, empty cigarette packages and dumped the ashtrays left there by drunken poets. And the whole thing would start over again, most of our time spent on the deck, begging Galloway to tell another story ... until he got a phone call.

He looked at the caller ID, looked at me, and flipped open his phone. Watching Joe move to a quieter location, I couldn't help but remember that this *was* Memorial Day and a little over a year ago Joe was in the same place, my deck, when he got that 'coming home' call. My writer friends kept talking. I listened for any sign of tears from Galloway. Instead, I heard him say, "Aw, thank you. It was mighty nice of you to call."

Suzanne was in the middle of a typical explanation of what she really meant five minutes ago when Galloway walked toward us, saying into the phone, "There's someone I want you to say 'hello' to," and handed me the phone. I asked who it was but apparently, so had the caller.

Galloway said, "It doesn't matter who the hell it is. Just say hello."

In the three seconds I had before greeting my unknown caller, I tried to recall the rank of General Hal Moore, sure it would be him and wanting to address him properly. Instead, I heard an unmistakable voice.

"Hello?" said Sam Elliott.

It has been well documented that I will step aside and give up any chance at George Clooney or Brad Pitt. Any woman who wants him can have Kevin Costner, Mel Gibson, or Denzel. I will take a gun totin', horse ridin', bad guy killin' cowboy anytime and have scolded Galloway on many, many occasions, that if he were any kind of decent friend to me, I would have long ago met Sam Elliott.

I apologized to Sam for being forced on the phone with a total stranger and he said, "To you, too. Joe didn't give you much choice, now, did he?"

Yeah, how cruel.

I told Sam that I much appreciated his taking on the voice role of Smokey the Bear as I was a very busy woman and him being Smokey saved me a lot of time. He asked how that was and I explained that I had loved Smokey since childhood, that my grandmother sent off for me to be an Official Park Ranger and they mailed me a coloring book and a badge and an autographed picture of Smokey.

"Since you became Smokey the Bear, I don't have to spend extra time loving you individually. I can love you collectively."

I made Sam Elliott laugh.

He told me that he had discovered some time after taking the voice role, he and Smokey shared a birthday, the same date and year. He thanked me for looking after Joe Galloway and I told him while that did require considerable effort, taking care of Joe's sorry ass, it was in fact an honor, and handed the phone back to Galloway.

He was standing on my deck.

I don't think I will be so embarrassed about not having a wraparound porch anymore. I believe I will work on accepting that as a change that is just fine and not because I got to stand on its boards and talk to a good lookin' movie star.

It is where Joe Galloway got the call that let one more part of that war be over, done. Those boys came home. Joe would go to Arlington to be there when they buried them, together, in American soil at last. My deck is where Bay Woods told of a violent carpet installer and the addiction counselor who got stoned and tore up commitment papers, a story that made Galloway laugh so hard it started to worry me. My deck is where my son sat and listened to Joe answer question after question, answers Walker knew were real and true, not from any history book but from one who was there, from the one who took on the job of telling all of us what really happened, how bad it really was. My deck is where Galloway sat with a local veteran of the Vietnam war and allowed him to talk, exchanged a couple of stories and gave a former medic something to brag about, his time with The Great Joe Galloway, and maybe a chance to heal, at least a little. My deck is where I talked to Sam Elliott and as fine lookin' and soundin' man as he is, that is not what matters in this story.

In this time of drugged out movie stars and celebrities who are famous for being famous, reality shows that offer no story line, no lesson, no entertainment but to humiliate its own cast, in this era of screaming insults on Fox News and American Idol, Sam Elliott called Joe Galloway on Memorial Day to thank him for his service. He also called General Moore, and Sergeant Major Basil Plumley—the role Elliott played in *We Were Soldiers.*

He thanked them, too.

We've got heroes. They're just harder to find. Once a year or so, you can find one of them at my house. He might be upstairs in his guest room writing commentary for CNN that reminds us to take a moment away from the grill and remember our veterans. He might be sitting at my dining room table explaining the Korean War to my son and his pretty girlfriend. He might be at the Back Table of the Claremont Café laughing his fool ass off, being one of *Them*, sure as the world, one of Them. He might be with other writers, a glass in one hand, a cigarette in the other, rocking in a chair no one else sat in even when he wasn't there. It was sacred. We knew it without speaking of it. It was Galloway's, Joe Galloway's chair on my deck.

It's where he was sitting when he got a call from another hero, not because he makes movies or gives a voice to a fire fightin' bear, not even because he takes good care of his momma. (Galloway told me that.) But because whatever it was he was doing on this Memorial Day, Sam Elliott stopped to call three men, three that we know of, and said "Thank you."

I know because one of those calls came in to my deck.

TWENTY-FIVE MINUTES

There came a day when our conscience moved to Texas.

All these Facebook posts and pictures come scrolling down in front of our eyes telling us that we are, each one of us, special and wonderful and uniquely necessary. You'd think we all deserve to be cast in bronze and stood on the courthouse square for all to read on the plaque welded to the pedestal we're perched upon, that the world would be a sorrier place had we not been born. Somewhere along the way, we forgot that we're supposed to actually do something to warrant living on in the memories of those left behind, and the stories they tell. We have forgone a life of service for typing our opinions on a social media feed and calling it a day, and we feel good about it. There was a time when it took good works to be remembered.

In the South, the sorry are remembered, too, but only for being sorry.

When Russell Boggs lived in Claremont, we all lived better. We behaved better. Not me, so much. I walked around in sin and swear words with his full blessing and to this day, I don't really know why. There are things that have happened in our town that would not have ever come to be had Russell been able to stay with us and not had to move to Texas for his health and Mary's mind. Folks did not want to disappoint him or they didn't want to lose his approval, or maybe it was just respect and the hope we could be a little more like him, and for all the love and hero worship and admiration we bestowed upon him, he believed he had married a woman with a soul far better than his.

I saw Mary today.

She is a woman who, at the height of the Civil Rights movement, got on a bus in Montgomery and took a seat in the back. I wanted to tell that story to the young black woman dressed in purple scrubs pushing a man in a wheelchair past where Mary sat, quietly turning the pages in a church bulletin. I wanted to ask her if she knew who it was she helped dress and shower every day. Instead, I walked across the floor, knelt and said, "Mary, it's me. It's Shari. Do you remember me?"

The mind is a funny, crazy thing. For all that is lost to her, gone from the life lived by Mary Boggs, the full and wonderful life of service to the world around her and love for Russell, she has not forgotten her manners. Even as she smiled at me, out of polite kindness, not from any sort of recognition, I knew in that instant this is what I would tell The Great Margaret Garrison, that Mary is still a Southern lady. Her sense of what is proper has not abandoned her and I was grateful, relieved not to have to grieve for it.

She said I looked familiar but that she had difficulty, that is what she said, "difficulty," remembering things. I said, "Me too." Mary laughed a little and said, "Then I am sorry for you and sorry for me."

I grabbed the arm of the chair to keep steady, seeing her laugh, hearing her make a joke. She used to laugh like that at the way I tormented Russell. It all flooded back with the sound of her voice.

"Mary, I am from Claremont. I was…"—and I wondered if it was the right thing to say—"I was Russell's friend."

Light shone in her face as she said, "Yes. The library."

And I could hold them no more. The tears came and they came to Mary, too. All I could choke out was, "Yes. Yes, Mary, the library. We did good, didn't we?"

She said we did. Mary asked me to tell her about "all the people back in that town. I so want to hear about them," but the first few folks I mentioned brought no sign of recognition. I will spare them from knowing who they are, but it struck me as just, that some of them deserve to be forgotten.

The first name she recognized was Katie Carpenter. I asked her if she remembered that she had given Katie the vest she had from the Lions Club. Mary said she didn't remember, but she was glad she did that. I told her Katie was as pretty as ever and had a nice boyfriend. Mary said she was glad about that, too. She asked me to tell her hello, "from Mary Boggs," she said.

I helped her take a Kleenex from her pocket. She said I needed a chair, that kneeling couldn't be comfortable for me and I thought of every cup of tea she served me in a china cup on a pretty tray. I told her I would rather be this close to her than to sit in a stupid ol' chair, and she laughed again.

I asked her if she remembered Edie Connor and could see that something sounded familiar. "What about Charlie? C-3? Do you remember him?" And she smiled and said, "Oh yes. I do. How is his family?" I told her Charles Franklin was getting married and that Catie had a baby boy named Eli. She said that was a beautiful name, "an old name, too, from a long time ago." I said it sure was.

I told her that Gaye Morrison was gardening and that Mayor Glenn was only working two or three days a week and doing yard work the rest of the time. I told her he wasn't the mayor anymore but everyone wished he was. Mary said, "They have a beautiful yard, I imagine." I told her that the people who live in her house love it very much and take good care of all their flower gardens, and she smiled the same way she did when I touched a memory. I knew she was seeing them, the hollyhocks, the foxgloves, the day lilies, and the ferns.

Mary said, "Do you know that he died?"

I said I did. "I spoke at his funeral, Mary. He wanted me to, so I did." Mary said, "Yes, you tell stories."

She wanted me to say hello to everyone, to tell "all the people in that town" that she hoped they could come and see her. She said she was sorry to have such a bad time remembering and that she was thankful I had come to her. I told her I would come again.

And when I hugged her, she hugged me back. I said, "I love you, Mary. I do." Mary said, "And I love you. Thank you for coming."

I was there for twenty-five minutes.

They are twenty-five minutes that were gone from her memory before I made it to the lobby. They are twenty-five minutes that will remain in my own.

Margaret Garrison is right about everything. She always has been, as far as I can tell. When we put Russell in the ground she called to see if I was coping or needed to be placed in a rubber room. Margaret said, "There is no more reason for Mary to be here one more minute. None. She needs to go to sleep and go to Russell."

I wish that were her call. I wish she were in charge. I have always worshipped The Great Margaret Garrison.

That is a church I would attend.

I went to a museum today. I saw works of sculpture and paint held in frames and on canvas, images of The West, of history. I don't have the gift of the visual arts. I can't draw a damn thing. Let this be written well enough that the next nurse who walks by Mary Boggs knows what she did for the rights of others. Let this find its way to someone who will remember that she lived a life that deserves to be remembered even if she has forgotten most of it. Let Macy, back in Claremont, now a teenager, know that Mary Boggs read her a story when she was a little girl, that she sat with a heroine, someone who changed the world for the better.

And let Claremont know, let Claremont remember, to send Mary a card and write happy, sunny things, for she is still Mary. She still laughs when something strikes her as funny. She still sits with her hands folded in her lap as all proper Southern women do. She still reads and she still feels, and I still believe that Russell is never far away.

I felt him there.

ANDREA, ME, AND A PACK OF SOUTHERN WOMEN

I first met Jefferson when we were coordinating an appearance for a writer. Jefferson was coming from Charlotte and I from Claremont, so Mooresville, home of NASCAR Teams and the only Steak and Shake in three counties fell closest to the middle. We were friends in an instant. We were far more four hours later when we said goodbye.

We could finish each other's sentences mostly because we were talking in movie lines and we loved the same ones. *Steel Magnolias* topped the list. We went through more napkins than the waitress could bring us, wiping tears of laughter as we exchanged stories of Southern women in hair salons, the practice of taking casseroles to the families of the dead but not before writing your name on a piece of tape and sticking it to the bottom of the Pyrex dish on account of wanting it back after the burial, and our favorite Southern phrases.

Jefferson's is "from off," as in, "Oh, you might not would know him.

He's from off."

Yesterday, the elected officials of a state whose very name makes me a tiny bit weepy decided that it is fine for me to get married no matter how many times I have proven my profound lack of good judgment in that regard, but Jefferson cannot.

David Williams and I rode in the back of Deb Cooper's show dog van, balancing on bags of Purina stacked five high, being stared at by Shar Peis from their travel crates, while Cooper broke speed limits in a vain attempt to get where we were going so she could escape the woman riding shotgun, the woman who endlessly chatted about her hobbies of restoring rocking horses and researching Navajo Indian weaving techniques. David and I clung to one another, not so much to avoid being thrown into the side walls of the van but in a desperate attempt to quiet our nearly hysterical laughter. Witnessing Cooper, a Chicago girl, never met a diamond she didn't like girl, a girl who did not/does not/will never own a pair of sensible shoes, nod politely while driving like a maniac and fake an interest in paint scraping and ancient tribal patterns, was nigh on more than we could take and remains strong enough in my memory to make me laugh out loud in the grocery store five years later when I see a bag of dog food and think of it.

Months later, I would go to the post office box I had to rent and find a check for $500 from folks calling themselves the Southern Handlers Charity League or something similar. I think there was a note telling me how sorry they were about my fire and hoping that the money would help, at least a little. There was no name. There was no single person claiming credit. No one in the dog world I asked knew who they were or where they came from. Only last week did I see a Facebook post from David listing the good works done by the Southern Handlers Charity League. They did not use my name because that would be against a Southern sense of manners. All it said was "a person in the dog community who lost everything in a fire."

David. I might should have known.

Those high and mighty legislators in Raleigh have decided that I am deserving of a right that David will be denied should he ever move to Carolina and fall in love.

When did it happen? Was I just not paying good attention? When did people who live in a country made up of every conceivable heritage and belief suddenly start deciding that their way was the only way.

I'm paying attention now.

Some wrote that they were ashamed of our state. Some wrote that it was a bad day to be from North Carolina. Some wrote that they were ready to go.

But, I'm stayin' and I'm keeping Andrea Busbee right here with me. She's got a smart husband and a good family but my money's on Andrea in this dog fight.

Andrea is crazy smart. She's so smart that it is a tiny bit hard for her to fake her way through dealing with those less endowed with gray matter. That makes me laugh. I could make a morning's entertainment out of watching her in the drugstore, that look on her face. Andrea requires a fair amount of caffeine and more than a healthy dose of intelligence just to get through the day. Sometimes, she only gets the coffee.

See, Andrea and I are gonna fix this. We're gonna call on the history of Southern women who, after finally taking all they could take, got fed up and fixed whatever was wrong. They ran the Underground Railroad, sat at the back of the bus if they were white and refused to go to the back of the bus if they were black until someone decided that they'd better stop acting like a jackass or find a way to live without biscuits and sex, not necessarily in that order.

Don't blame this current bunch of horseshit on the South. Don't blame it on the country South.

I knew a woman, not a tooth in her head, who rented a house to two gay boys who collected beanie babies and groomed dogs and decorated to perfection. I was standing in her garden one day when one of them came walking across the yard. A crate had fallen on him, tearing open a gash in his back. He was bleeding horribly. She saw him and quickened her pace among the chickens running wild. He held up his hand and lowered his head. He told her to stop, not to come near him. He asked her to go in the house and see if she had anything he could use for bandages, just enough to stop the bleeding so he could get to the hospital.

I understood. I spent fifteen years in the big city. I understood. I wondered if she did.

"Hush," she said. "I don't care nuthin' 'bout your ol' AIDS."

I watched that woman, without anything more than a fourth grade education, put on a pair of Playtex dish washing gloves. She cleaned him while reminding him that she had told him to be more careful. I don't think she stopped fussing at him the entire time she tended to his back. When his partner came to fetch him, tote him to the hospital, she said, "You s'pose I need to go, n'case that doctor tries to be mean to y'all?"

She is my people.

My cousin, who has Tennessee red mountain clay running through her veins, said it best. "You don't agree with gay marriage? Don't have one." My agent, in a pissed off rant said, "Exactly what do they mean, they don't *believe* in gay marriage? Well, guess what? I can say I don't believe in pine trees but there they are."

Eudora Welty, a proper Southern woman who had her own recipe for pecan pie and mint juleps and wrote many of the Southern classics, enjoyed a long and happy friendship with Reynolds Price, a man who preferred to be called "queer," as he thought that was funnier. His own writing was elegant. Miss Eudora thought so. I talked to him on the phone once. There is only one word, lovely. He was lovely, and when he died this past year North Carolina grieved, as well we should. He belonged to us, to these hills, to this place. Sometimes I look at his picture and wonder if he would have thought I was any good at this writing thing. It doesn't really matter. Still, I wonder.

Sometimes.

Nelle Harper Lee spent her childhood protecting a slight, oddly dressed little boy named Truman Capote, and defended him in adulthood even when he didn't deserve it. *Breakfast at Tiffany's, In Cold Blood, The Grass Harp*—my favorite—all written by a gay man who was first befriended by a Southern girl, a Southern woman who would ask all the questions that needed to be ask, say all the things that had to be said, and put in the pages of one book all that we need to know about how to treat each other; that walking around in another man's skin was the only way to know what his life was like. She wrote the book to which all other books are compared and always, always fall short.

Miss Nelle knew a thing or two about looking for mockingbirds. She was right. It is a sin to kill them. They do nothing but make music, write books, paint, draw, laugh, cry, love, live...just like the rest of us.

It's a fine line to walk, to criticize, to question something and love it so very much. I continue to love my Carolina, my South. I know we were wrong yesterday, that the rights of one are the rights of all. Anyone who does not agree with gay marriage is free to go to a church with like-minded people and exclude anyone they wish. A government cannot, must not. I believe that Andrea and I will see it change. She and Scott are fifteen years younger than I, so they may have to pick up the charge if I wear out, but I believe their daughter, London, will grow up to wonder what all the fuss was about, that in her lifetime no one will ask and everyone will tell because it finally dawns on people that it just doesn't matter who is sleeping with whom.

It really doesn't.

If you want something to worry about, how about this: let's forget about those neighbor boys who hope to get married someday soon and both wear white lace and pumps. Let's wish them well, along with their maid of honor, the one with the five o'clock shadow. In fact, let's go to the wedding because if one stereotype is true it is that gay boys can dance. You have not lived until you've seen them hit the dance floor when the deejay plays "I'm Every Woman."

Now I don't care who you are, that is funny.

Instead, let's worry about the neighbor down the other way, the one who has cancer but no health insurance since getting laid off down at the mill. Let's fret over the children who keep coming to school saying they "forgot" their lunch money, or their coats, even as the temperatures dip. Let's say we'll get together and find a way to save a home, just one, in our town as the bank threatens to take it away from the couple who bought it not knowing they'd run out of work long before they ran out of bills. Let's worry about the man we haven't seen at The Café in a few days, the baby who the doctors said would not live but did, the man who walks the streets and talks to the bushes, the nice lady trying to run the store by herself. Let's worry about that.

And, if I were all y'all on the wrong side of this, I might would worry about me and Andrea—cause in the words of *Tombstone*, baby, "You tell 'em I'm coming and hell's coming with me."

THE PEOPLE YOU MEET THEY ALL SEEM TO KNOW YOU

The pretty young mother, her babe held tight against her in a sling and covered over with her momma's coat, all but yelled across a fire pit and over the music of the guitars being played. She wanted to be heard.

"This is all I have ever known, these people, these wonderful people, hanging out at my parents' house. I guess it's true that you're more emotional after you have a baby, but it makes me so proud that she will grow up the same way, surrounded by all this love. Really, that's what it is, just love. It's all love."

I said it sure seemed to be...but I didn't know that I was talking to a mermaid.

Some folks think I've run away from home. My cousin thinks I'm in need of an intervention, which done Tennessee hill people style, means whuppin' somebody's ass—if not mine—anybody who has hurt my tender little feelings along the road. Folks back in Claremont are gossiping.

"She's run off."

"Naw, she's comin' back."

"Ain't so. She's left for good."

I've hit six states in four months.

I've eaten Renee's macaroni and cheese in The Holler, catfish in Memphis, sliced brisket in Fort Worth, a shrimp po'boy in Monroe, Louisiana, Hudson's gumbo along Mobile Bay, and elk chili in Aripeka, Florida—the elk having covered more miles than me. I listened to a man who is more my brother than my friend sing in three states and a guitar god play in three more. Michael Reno Harrell told a Christmas story in February under the moss of the live oaks, and a man I did not know sang of the hurricane who was his gone brother, while the wind blew the palm trees as if they could hear him, too. I counted sixty-four hawks and two bald eagles in less than six hours of driving, and was told of marshmallow eating gators in the Delta. By the time I am home, I will have seen the tarpon of Key West I could only watch jumping on my television screen in the documentary I've seen a hundred times.

It might be easy to think only of the bad. My beloved horse died. Somebody who needed a battery more than a clear conscience smashed in my car window and popped the hood. A woman who said she needed my help and offered her own, skipped out on bills and left the sheets thrown back on the bed, feeling good I suppose that she'd washed them. I watched a man prove what he is made of pay a price that was nearly too high to survive, and I learned that there are some languages I will never speak and don't much care to.

But there was Lucy.

Lucy laughed with me and when I couldn't, she at least didn't cry. Lucy talked of messages from the universe and almost made me believe. Lucy, who feeds stray cats and makes weavings of guitar strings, walked into the BBQ joint my last night in Texas, throwing back her shawl and stretching out her arms in a "*ta-da*" that would shame the best of magicians, to present her sense of honor as she had indeed invited a man on a date I was sure would offer her true love, and if not that then a really good time; and I laughed until I cried.

And when I said I was leaving Texas, Lucy, because she chooses love over selfishness, said, "Good."

There was Deedee who collects crosses and loves Jesus and thinks

He wasn't kidding around when He said, "Judge not." Deedee and I could clap at the end of every song the band played and never lose our place in a conversation that we barely needed as we could read each other's mind. She knows what is important and what is not. That is harder to find than it should be and I will miss that.

There was Patrick. We live on opposite sides of the political spectrum and chose friendship, chose love, over philosophical differences. Also, we both really love pie.

There was Diane. I didn't get enough time with her but what time I spent was like talking to an old friend. We both really love mashed potatoes.

There was a man named Greg and his wife, named Kristie, who paid attention when others talked. I noticed because so many others had not. They looked into the faces of the person talking and actually listened. That's love, too, I think, or at least a sort of kindness, to really listen.

Then came Robert.

He had read my stories and knew I had walked on Sacred Ground. We laughed over how our people write their names on masking tape and stick them to the bottom of Pyrex dishes when bringing food to families of the deceased, because no matter how sorry they are about your dead aunt, they really want that pie plate back when y'all are through grieving. His boyfriend bought me a margarita and pretended we were family before we actually were. We are now, Robert, my Brother Boy, me, his Sister Girl, so I reckon that makes Randy my brother-in-law, which is the way Andrea Busbee and me think it should be. He knew that on account of he read that story too.

It is the love I will remember from that time. It's easy for me. It's my nature, to throw out the hate even when I should keep track of at least a little of it, if only to protect myself should it come around again. I'm better than I used to be at that, which isn't saying much. I don't care for the numbness of protective layers between me and the people I meet. I feel pretty lucky when all is said and done. I'll keep taking my chances.

Some of my Carolina people came to me. Shelley Setzer got on a plane and brought me a bracelet, in memory of my horse, and her fine company for three whole days. We got our picture made while laughing while Shelley was pretty drunk. When the weekend was over we loved the same people and didn't much care for the same people, which made it fun to spend one night late, two weeks later, on the phone, again laughing like we didn't have good sense. Michael and Joan Harrell traveled the ribbon of road that will lead me back to cheeseburgers at The Café, with Michael's lie that he hadn't eaten lunch since I left and Joan's list of spring time garden plans using the book I gave her for her last birthday. I missed them two minutes after they left for the land and the people I know, the people I am.

Hudson hugged me when I got back to Alabama. Hudson ain't a hugger. I must have looked like someone had shot my dog. I didn't look that way for all that long.

I met Diane Floyd. She is an artist, interested in birds, in books, in home design, in music, in cooking, in laughing. Pretty sure we'll have some fun. I met a guitar player named Robbie who sang a Bob Dylan song unknown to me. I met a drummer named Geno who should have his own comedy channel and played "Little Wing" with Chris better than any other drummer, ever, and I have heard quite a few. When I rushed the stage past Chris to hug that drummer's neck and tell him so, he said the first serious thing I had heard come out of his mouth: "I've never had anything happen like that in my whole life. Can you imagine how we'd sound if we'd, maybe, practiced?"

On the Alabama-Florida line, I met a sound man who knew his way around a stage and all those blinking green and red lights, who said, when he learned I was a writer, "I like knowing famous people. They are more interesting."

I met a roadie who, when he saw me get hit in the mouth by a guitar swung over a shoulder at the exact moment I walked by, said, "You sure can take a punch, Cowgirl." He said it real sweet.

With my sore jaw, I got in the car and rode to the middle of the Sunshine State listening to the list of people I was soon to meet, knowing I wouldn't remember who was who, and watching for hawks and hoping for eagles.

I got creatures far more rare and beautiful.

In all my life, now in it's fifth decade, I have not known people of such warmth. I wish to all that is holy I could claim them as native Southerners, but truth be told, there is a good bit of Ohio and I might could have heard Minnesota mentioned, but I blocked that out. Only good souls could create a place like this, a home that feels good the moment you walk in, a nest where even the other guests are offering you a seat, a drink, and a bowl of chili; where everybody hugs and means it, where the baby is eyeballed like a flank steak at a dog kennel, because everyone is trying to get their hands on her to chew on her cheeks and kiss on the back of her baby neck. They value the guests who come to visit so much they have built cottages with comfy beds and big screen televisions, and stoves and refrigerators and a shower that looks like the spa you can't never afford to join. It even came with a little lizard just to make sure we knew we were in Florida.

When I was a child watching Flipper and Gentle Ben on my Papaw's Zenith console television I used to daydream about traveling on an airboat, those flat bottom things with an oversized window fan on the back, and having a bear and a dolphin for pets. Today I rode on an airboat for the very first time. My captain's name was Ron. He navigated through the saw grass that formed the channels and paths for the boat, skimming the surface of water no deeper in places than the "Jungle Safari" ride at Disney World. I could see the bottom and the fish that swam in hurried scatters to avoid the wake of the boat. Instead of plastic elephants spewing water from their fiberglass trunks, I saw egrets and cranes, and an osprey that used the wind to rest its wings as it sailed over palms that looked like giant, top-heavy dandelions—waiting for a child to pluck them from the shallow water and blow their seeds into the sky. I watched two buzzards sitting in a dead tree as if they weren't welcome or comfortable among the living. The captain pointed to ferns growing in patches every now and then and told us that they only grow where fresh water springs from the ground. He used to take his children, his girls, swimming there.

That's how one of them became a mermaid.

Her name is Karri. Tomorrow, I will see her give up her legs and don a tail and breathe under water.

She called it "Old Florida," and that reminded me of my great-grandfather coming every winter, his daughter, my grandmother driving him down and taking the train home, stopping at Cypress Gardens to watch the ski shows and the Bok Singing Tower and a swan that chased me when I was too young to know they didn't take to being petted. Karri swims with the Weeki Watchee World Famous Mermaids. Her long blond hair floats up and around the costume her momma and sister told me she painted herself. She makes an air hose look like a magic wand so the children, and maybe me too, can believe that there is a world under the sea, a place of princes and witches and pretty mermaids all in a row.

She named her baby Koral.

When I remember this time, these months away from Claremont where I have spent the last seventeen years of my life, the best years for certain, I will think of Karri. I am sure of it. There was Lucy and Deedee and the folks who appreciate a good piece of pie, which is really any piece of pie, and a helping of mashed potatoes, and those who paid attention, and there was Robert. There was a drummer and a sound guy and a roadie who called me Cowgirl, and an artist and more that came and went for a minute or an hour, but never long enough. There is a boat captain and his wife, whom I want to know better for she is the mother of a mermaid named Karri and Karri is the one who helped me see.

This place, this earth, my South, is made up of wonderful people, the people you meet. I can spend all kinds of time searching for the words to describe them, but it's really just love. It's just love. It's a little bit of tequila, sure, but it's love. Some folks are better at showing it. They trust that language while others think they can hide their pain in a suit of mean and a coat of hateful, but they're just lonely. I am sad about that. I choose to be sad about that but not angry. I choose this place, this place of love.

It's just love.

If from time to time I forget that, I'm going to find a mermaid and asked her to remind me.

OUR UNPLEASANT JOBS

Nearly everybody's read it even if they don't remember the line in *To Kill A Mockingbird*: "...there are some men in this world who were born to do our unpleasant jobs for us." In Claremont, our man was P.J. Stanley.

Folks are busy this sad day, looking up dates when P.J. was born, when he joined the police force, the rescue squad, the fire department, was elected to the city council. They're calling Pam down at the police station to find out what time to show up for services, where to go. Tom Winkler is lowering city flags and trimming hedges so the wreaths we hang will show better. The women of this town are cooking enough food to feed both Carolinas and half of Georgia and the men at the Back Table of the Claremont Café are shaking their heads and not talking as much as usual, except to repeat themselves and what they know about why a good man is gone.

Gail Carpenter said, "He can't be gone. He saved my daddy's life one time." And that is how it feels. He can't be gone. Who will save a daddy's life, talk a Saturday night drunk into putting down the bottle and coming peacefully, decide who gets Claremont Yard of the Month, organize the drop off stations for expired prescriptions, convince folks they need reflective house numbers because first responders really can't see in the dark, or lead the city council meetings in the Pledge of Allegiance?

He can't be gone.

There are books in a library in Grand Isle, Louisiana because P.J. Stanley decided they ought to be there. He always went to the places where people needed him the most. When a mean hurricane with a pretty name tore roofs and flooded schools, P.J. found a town that reminded him of ours and brought back the idea that we adopt them, tend to them with clothes and food and insulation and Christmas trees. They came to thank us, their mayor, their leaders, their preacher. P.J. took them to a spaghetti dinner in a barn in the mountains and gave them such a welcoming, they had more to thank him for when they left than they did when they got here.

He can't be gone.

In my ten years of friendship with P.J. Stanley, he mowed my yard, helped me haul a broken dishwasher to the street, pulled a piece of metal out of the mower deck of my John Deere, jump-started my car, loaned me a Sawzall, taught me how to use a Sawzall, rewired a drop cord I'd cut in two with a Sawzall, and put me on a committee with a representative from each of the five churches in town. "Somebody's gotta be here for the backsliders, Shari," he said when he grinned at me.

And, nearly three years ago, he stood by my side while a fire took a house I loved. He ran to small, meaningless blazes with a garden hose because I would point to them, believing getting them gone would save a house engulfed in flames. He'd come back and tell me he'd gotten it good and out, because for a few minutes I felt better, and when I was ready to hear it, he is the one person I turned to for the truth. "I believe it's gone," he said. There is not another man I would have believed. In the nearly three years since that day, since I moved a couple of blocks away, he never stopped calling me neighbor. He never stopped saying that he missed seeing me across that street.

And now, he's gone.

I slumped in a chair and listened to the police chief say, "Folks in other places don't understand that around here when we say we lost a friend, we mean we lost family." That is true. I watched the chief slip a black band around his badge. I thought how odd it was that in all the times I saw P.J. in a uniform I never thought of him as a policeman, though he certainly was one. I never thought of him as an EMT or a firefighter or, truth be told, I never thought of him as a city councilman. I only knew him to be family. His beloved Brenda shared him with all of us, with this town. I hurt for her and their blended family and the grandchildren I saw him toss in the air. I hurt for all of us. I hurt for me.

Margaret Garrison always tends to see the good in things, which can be downright irritating when you just feel like pitching a fit. She said it best today, right there in the beauty parlor, and even a backslider knows the truth when it's spoken in a sea of hair color and hot wax.

"Thank God we knew him."

GROWING UP
IN PRIVILEGE

Walker asks a lot of questions.

For most parents there is some end to the "why" age, a break in the endless line of inquiry as to why your favorite color is black and why you like German Shepherd dogs better than other dogs, and why you like dogs more than cats and why your name is spelled funny.

Not for me.

When Walker says he wants to talk, he really means he wants to ask questions. He will ask why my favorite defensive football player of all time is Ronnie Lott, and then ask why my favorite current player is Peyton even though he, too, worships at the altar of St. Manning, and then ask if I absolutely had to choose between Ronnie and Peyton, which one would I say is my favorite football player. Then, he'll ask why. Why did I love the combination of John Stockton and Karl Malone? Why do I say Hudson's second novel is my favorite but most often recommend her first? Why do I say Jackson Browne is my favorite songwriter but listen more often to James Taylor? Really? Well, then, why do I listen to

James Taylor more often when he is in the house or in the car? Really? Then, why do I *think* I might be doing that? Well, why do I think *he* thinks I do that?

"Mom, why are you getting mad?"

He was twenty in November.

A couple of years ago, I looked outside the bank of kitchen windows to see Walker talking to Joe Galloway, author of *We Were Soldiers...Once and Young*, the book named one of the top ten books on war. Walker was leaning forward, arms resting on his legs, and I knew. Joe, a hard-nosed old school newspaper man had never in his storied career asked more questions than he was, at that moment in time, having to answer. Walker and six of his buddies had chosen Joe's book to read for an assignment in their English class. Now, he had the horse's mouth captive in his own back yard.

I watched Joe gesturing and rocking back in his chair, looking to the sky, pointing at Walker, laughing, clapping, twisting his hands while he talked. He was enjoying being grilled by this kid who wanted to understand exactly what he meant in the writing of every paragraph, this kid who wanted to know "why."

Walker came inside and opened the 'fridge. As he searched for the Sundrop, he said, "How cool is this? I mean, like, how cool is this? People are always talkin' shit like they know everything about stuff, but I am talking to the guy who was there. I mean, he was really there. He's, like, a total badass. This is cool."

It really was.

Later, over dinner, he launched another inquisition. I knew we were in for it when, as he laid his plate on the table, he said, "Mr. Joe, I never really understood the Korean War. Why did all that happen?"

They sat at the table until well after dark. I didn't know Galloway could go that long without a cigarette.

The next day, Joe Formichella was chopping, doing the prep work for my paella. Walker and his friend, Nick, sat at the kitchen island and asked questions. Mostly Walker asked questions. Joe wrote a book on a basketball coach. Before dinner was served, Walker could have written a book on how Joe wrote the book. I would have considered slitting my wrist with the serrated edge of the bread knife, except it was a thing not to miss, a moment in time when I could be there and invisible, just listen and watch the way one answer led Walker to another question, and Joe's excitement at being asked such meaningful questions.

When everyone was gone the day next, Walker said, "Of all the writers who come here and hang out, Joe Formichella is my favorite. He's just cool. I like everyone but Joe is my favorite. Also, when he and Suzanne come, they always bring the leftovers from the restaurants where they ate on the way here and they never take them when they leave."

Then he pulled a chicken enchilada from the Styrofoam box and tossed it in the microwave.

He can perform a flawless impersonation of Bay Woods shaking hands, meeting someone. When I insisted he do so for Formichella, Joe laughed so hard he had to sit down. Bay, the editor of *City Paper* in Baltimore, and author of *Coffin Point* with Formichella and an editor from Montgomery and one from Raleigh, played basketball against a team of Walker's friends.

One question Walker does not ask, ever, is "Are writers good athletes?"

He trapped Texan Chris Clifton in the kitchen for an afternoon covering the history of the Dallas Cowboys and the Texas Rangers. A week later, they were in the living room for hours, locked in a back and forth on all-things-guitar. He came into my room later and sat on the bed, a look that combined disgust and shock and amazement on his face. He said, "Mom, why, I mean, really...*why* didn't you tell me that Chris had been on the same stage with Jimmy Page? Jimmy Page? Really? I mean, really, James Taylor, Jimmy Buffett, and a shit-ton of other people, but Jimmy Page? You didn't think that was important to tell me?"

I really didn't.

My question is, "what is a shit-ton?"

After a long conversation with musician/story teller Michael Reno Harrell, Walker got in his car and drove off to hang with friends. I don't know what they talked about. All Michael said was, "God, that is a good kid. He certainly knows how to hold up his end of a conversation."

A Pulitzer Prize winner sat on his front porch when he was in the fourth grade. His kitchen table has been a revolving party of "the guy who wrote the book," literally and liter—ar—ily. A man who wrote a twelve page story on some kind of fish which I have mercifully forgotten talked to him about what trout were native to North Carolina and which ones were trucked in and dumped in our rivers. Roy Williams autographed a copy of his autobiography to Walker for Christmas, thanking him for loving the Tarheels, which he does more than he loves his momma, but not more than he loves asking questions, though it's close.

Two nights ago, late, really late, I got a text message from Walker. He said he was instant messaging on the computer with Joe Formichella. Walker asked if he could call me, if it was too late. When I answered the phone, he said that he had signed up for a baseball class in college, one hard to get into.

I would imagine so.

Walker said that he saw Joe online and asked him about the book he wrote on the Negro Baseball League, the one that hangs in the Hall of Fame in Cooperstown. Walker was taking notes for a debate on which player was the best to ever play in the league. He had chosen Satchel Paige, said Joe told him he had chosen well. He said that he was getting all kinds of good information from Joe.

I would imagine so.

After I hung up from Walker, I got an email from Joe. He said he was locked in a session with Walker who was asking questions about baseball, a lot of questions. I laughed out loud. Walker says he is going to be a sports writer.

Joe thinks Walker is going to be a writer.

Walker has a shirt that Joe gave him. He left it for him because he knew Walker wouldn't accept it any other way. It was Joe's favorite shirt, the denim shirt with the patch of The Negro Baseball League. When I handed it to him, he was honored and embarrassed he hadn't gotten up in time to refuse it. "This is his favorite," he said.

Walker put on loose khaki shorts, a T-shirt, and a pair of Chuck Taylor tennis shoes. He put a hat on backwards, and slipped his long arms into the denim shirt Joe left for him. He was on his way to the Claremont Café.

He dressed like Joe.

There are some who think he would have been better served had he grown up in a million dollar home, one with the indoor pool, that Walker would have had a better life in a private school and rides in a Maserati to his basketball games. They paint his childhood as having been spent in the backwoods of the South where folks don't speak good English, where trucks are up on cinder blocks in the front yard, and the answer to "Can you come and help with the Fall Festival at the school?" is "I might could."

The truth is that he grew up in privilege. He ate at the Claremont Café with mill workers and a Bronze Star recipient who wrote *the* book on the Vietnam War. He stole his neighbor's chickens to set loose in the yard of the football coach and got to tell the story to a guy whose book hangs in Cooperstown, a guy who so loves him he gave him his favorite shirt. He's written rap with a kid he's known since kindergarten and talked music with the man called a "guitar god." The woman referred to as the Southern literary genius of our generation orders extra helpings on her way to his house so he will like her, at least a little bit as much as he does her husband.

And the guy who wrote the song Walker tortured his mother with for a solid three years, slept in a guest room and took a shower in his bathroom before he took the stage, a stage made from a flatbed wagon, to raise money for the library in that little town Walker grew up in.

I guess my real question is, how could it have been any better?

FORGIVENESS

Earlier this week, Matilda, over the phone, counted to thirty-eight in Spanish. Each of her parents separately posted to Facebook a photograph of her writing her letter to Santa without assistance. She is five. She is in kindergarten. Clearly she is brilliant and gifted beyond measure, and the most precious and perfect child that has been born in the last 2012 years.

Her momma sent me a text message today, a picture of Matilda in the back seat of the car, pulling the seat belt across her lap, smiling a sort of goofy, toothy grin—the long hair she waited so long to have going every way except the direction it's supposed to. From the other side of the country after today's tragedy, Abbie sent this to let me know that she had her, this smart and funny child, our smart and funny child.

Our five-year-old had survived a day at school.

I watched television all day like most everybody else, I reckon. I saw both our President and seasoned, hardened news anchors reduced to tears, unable to speak the words they needed to say to give us the news of what had happened. Lester Holt, of NBC, upon hearing that it was a kindergarten class that a gunman had walked into, opening fire on five-year-olds, grabbed the desk in front of him and said, his voice breaking in disbelief, "Kindergarteners?"

Kindergarteners.

If I had an ounce of sense I would stay out of the fray, the debate that began the minute the news hit. Folks just could not wait to weigh in on the issue of gun control, for and against and all points in between, as if any of this is about a gun. The most amazing to me were the ones claiming that if someone in the school had a concealed carry permit and was toting a gun somewhere between their lesson plan and their lunch box, they could have stopped the killing and saved lives.

Yes, just what we need, educators packin' heat.

My daddy didn't teach me to shoot and he's real sorry about that. I'm sorry, too. I would have liked to have learned from him. He was real good at it, won us lots of turkeys and hams when he kicked the asses of the other gun lovers at trap shooting matches, and he was the one to pull the trigger on butchering day when we offed about six hogs and nearly as many steers to put in the freezers of everyone in the family, and a few close friends. There was a gun case in the dining room, which I suppose is a little odd but I never thought so. I watched him clean them and load them and shoot them and hide them and pack them for hunting and fishing trips. I did not touch them because I was told not to. I know this; they never jumped from the gun cabinet and hopped in the Ford and drove on down to the school and shot anybody.

But, then, neither did anyone I ever heard of.

A friend of mine wrote a song that says "*something's wrong with the world.*" I've been wondering what it is all day long. I'm not the first to ask the question and not the first to be left without the answers, but whatever is wrong has been wrong for a long time, only now we have more channels dedicated to telling us about it.

I grieve for the families who lost today. I grieve for the parents who could not send text messages of their five-year-old to grandparents to say, "I've got her." I grieve for the family of the shooter, too. What nightmare of a life must he have lived, must they have lived with him, for this to be the only solution he could come up with. What demons must have haunted this young man, a boy the same age as my own son who can't stand to kill mice or spiders, or watch commercials showing dogs and cats in shelters waiting to be adopted, on account of his big, tender heart.

I grieve for him.

They say my great-grandmother was as crazy as a shithouse rat. I don't know. She died well before I was born. They say she cried a lot and I heard one story that had her standing over her youngest baby's crib with a butcher knife. Telling that story, over and over in front of my aunt, the baby in that crib, had made her a little nuts her own self. My great-grandmother was a poor woman who married a poor man and had five children. I have a very plain glass cake plate that belonged to her. My grandmother, her daughter-in-law, gave it to me and told me to take real good care with it, that "she didn't have many pretty things."

Her fourth child hanged himself minutes after my grandfather left, having surprised him with a visit to the business he owned. Nobody much knew why, or if they did they never would say. There was enough crazy in that next generation to keep the experts busy for a long time. They might could have coined the phrase "dysfunctional family" by hearing stories about my aunts and uncle and second cousins and my own mother. I wouldn't bet against it.

I had one uncle, the oldest of the family, who got gone and stayed gone even when a diving accident paralyzed him. He chose to live away from his family, to hire caretakers and depend on the generosity of friends. He had been a brilliant musician, could play any instrument handed to him. There are silent home movies of him when his legs and arms still worked fine, laughing so hard he was nearly hysterical over me.

I was on a rocking horse and I was singing, though you can't hear it in a 1962 eight-millimeter film. I was singing "You Are My Sunshine" but had pitched it too high and when I got to the *"you make me hap—PY,"* I couldn't hit it and so would start over, same key, same too-high key, and fail to hit it one more time. I don't remember him as whole. I only knew him in his chair, in his bed.

He taught me to read a map when I was five, same age that Matilda is now. He had a map of the world tacked to his wall, the wall of the tiny house he lived in far away from his family. On one visit, he showed me latitude and longitude, and though I famously don't understand numbers, I understood him. Looking back, I think he saw something in me. I think he thought I was different, different like him. I think we would have been close had the cancer not taken him away before I would turn nine.

But I got gone, too, and I stayed gone, and I understand him even if he did not live to explain himself to me.

I know that the mistakes I have made have hurt people and that, at the time, it seemed like it was the only way. That makes me different from the boy who did the shooting today only by degrees. Folks have called him evil. I don't think so. Maybe he was born with his hard wiring done up wrong.

Maybe he didn't know to get gone.

I cannot find it in myself to hate him—only to hate what he did. I cannot abide the excuse folks are using to fight on the Facebook about guns when that doesn't have a damn thing to do with what happened today. They were only his weapons of choice. He had a lot of choices in his weaponry. I'm sorry he felt resorting to guns was the only way.

I tend to be pretty good at forgiveness. Maybe it is because I feel I need it from so many I hurt or damaged when I should have known better. I have learned that forgiving doesn't mean hanging around for more. I still stay gone, but I don't wish for bad things to happen to those who damaged me. I don't care nor do I have enough time to bother with that. I have my own faults to tend to.

And I don't wish that boy had lived so we could hang him or strap him to a slab and stick a needle in his arm, or to a chair and flip the switch. I am glad he finally got gone and I hope there is some peace for him when he couldn't find any while he was here, as I am quite sure he already spent his time in hell.

I watched a video that Matilda's daddy sent to me a few weeks ago. She is on some kind of jungle gym, maybe at the park. She is singing "Happy Birthday" to me; "Happy Birthday, dear Lovie." Her hair is a mess. You can't look at her and not see how incredibly bright she is. It's been that way since she was born. Her momma has always talked to her as though she could understand her and so she did. She lets her pick out her own clothes, even if they don't match, and she tells her she is smart and beautiful and funny, and she is most certainly all of that.

Mostly, tonight, I am glad only that she is here.

I choose forgiveness and I understand if those whose Matildas and Jacks and Abbies and Walkers and Justins and Nates aren't here can't get there to that forgiving place for a long time, but I hope they do someday, for their own sakes, for their own souls. I hope they find peace. I imagine it is in very short supply tonight, and well out of their reach. God, that hurts me for them and I am glad of it.

I am glad I can feel something that deeply for other people. It separates me from the bad kind of crazy. I am sure of it. I am also sure that it might have been a different story had I not learned how to get gone. I might have never remembered how to read a map and find the right place to be, the safe place to go in a storm.

For me, that place is forgiveness.

A MARVEL-OUS NAME

I've been fighting pretty good with Chuck Cannon over which one of us has aunts with the best names. He thought he landed a body blow, some sort of Southern smackdown when he yelled in a false sense of triumph, "Well, *I* got an Aunt Willie Gus."

"Oh yeah? I got an Aunt Viney."

I used to take baths in a washtub she filled with water she heated on the stove after she pulled that tub close to the fire. Aunt Viney lived in Moss, Tennessee, where there ain't even a stoplight nor any call for one.

There was Aunt Jewel who was married to Uncle Les, the grandparents of my favorite cousin. Uncle Les could make a chicken go to sleep by turning it on its back and sort of rocking it in a circular motion. I thought it was a magical power harnessed only by Marqie's granddaddy but when I marveled at it here recently, my own daddy proclaimed that he could do it, too.

"You just ain't never seen me." He added, "But then..." and let it trail off like there was all kinds of good stuff I had missed.

I reckon so.

On the other side, I had four great-aunts, one the sister of my grand-mother, and four on Papaw's side. Mamaw's sister was named Cleo Gladys and my Papaw would send me into the "other room" at family dinners, the one where the womenfolk were hangin' out complaining as to the sorry men, and tell me to say, "I love you, Aunt Cleo Happy Bottom," to which she would squeal with laughter and slap her leg.

She always slapped her leg when she laughed. That was the payoff for doing like I was told because I was near grown before I got the joke.

Papaw's sisters were, from youngest to oldest, Blanche, Madge, and Marvel (take *that*, Cannon). Aunt Marvel was my favorite. She had blue hair and she jacked it up to Jesus. It was piled so high that her hairdresser had to pull it back down and around in two curls on each side of her head. Only recently have I seen any hairdo like it, and when I did I sent an emergency text message to Lucy Ford that said, "Get your ass over here. There's a woman who looks just like my Aunt Marvel. It shouldn't be missed."

Lucy requested to someday name a cat "Aunt Marvel," and because I adore Lucy I said she could.

Aunt Marvel sent me books in the mail, and occasionally clippings from the newspaper about folks tearin' the fire out of James Dean's headstone so they could take home their own little piece of the granite. She was the only woman who would cuss in front of me and she laughed at the jokes the men told, neither of which seemed to please my grand-mother. Aunt Marvel also chain-smoked and therefore had a voice like a redneck Bette Davis.

She was, in a word, glorious.

When my grandfather died in a farming accident, a death none of us would ever recover from, least of all my own daddy who loved him more like a father than a father-in-law, they lined the funeral home, twice around and out the door and down the sidewalk that was frozen solid from an ice storm. It did not deter many mourners. He was loved and respected and folks came from places we'd never heard of to tell my mamaw that her husband was good to plow the snow from their driveways after every storm, and never would take a dime for his trouble or diesel fuel. Aunt Marvel lived far enough away that she couldn't make The Calling and had to wait until the next day, the funeral day, to see that her brother really was dead, to stand at his casket and cry.

She cried hard.

We were already seated, the family, in our special section facing the congregation and the coffin where my grandfather was dressed in a suit he shouldn't have been in for eternity. My grandmother was in the middle of the first row with me to her right. My Uncle Don sat next to me. Aunt Marvel was his favorite, too, and when she went to pieces so did we.

She cried and clung to the casket and said, over and over, "My brother. Oh, my brother," so real it broke everybody's heart in two. I believe it was her grandson, my cousin, Roger, who had long hippie hair and was twelve years older than me and on whom I had suffered a lifelong crush, who helped her from my dead grandfather's side to her place in the second row directly behind us, the immediate family, and alongside of my Aunt Madge, with Aunt Blanche on her left.

The organ played "In the Garden" and "How Great Thou Art" for a man who didn't go to church a day in his life. We sniffed and wiped the tears we cried with my Aunt Marvel in her wrenching grief over the loss of her brother and the patriarch of our family.

I think it was during the chorus of "The Old Rugged Cross" when it all got good.

Not a one of them could hear, my great-aunts. They didn't seem to notice or thought nobody else could hear either so they whisper-yelled, and with Aunt Marvel's cigarette voice, she strained even harder to be heard.

"Blaaaanche. Blaaaannnnche."

I panicked.

My family suffers a common genetic ailment, a condition. Abbie has it, too, and has either passed it to her husband or married another one of the afflicted.

We have no control over socially inappropriate laughter.

Even in grief, we can just be gone and ain't nothing and ain't nobody could ever bring us back including the threat of grandmother's wrath who did not suffer from the affliction.

"Blaaaanche!" Aunt Marvel whisper-yelled.

"Whaaaatttt?" my Aunt Blanche hissed back at her.

I leaned away from my Uncle Don. He was a shaker. He married in and so had some level of control over volume but instead, shook, and I knew if I felt it, if I felt him shake, there was no hope for me.

"Did you get the flowers?"

"Whaaat?"

"DID YOU GET THE FLOWERS?"

I saw my Aunt Marianna put her hand to her mouth and I began to pray for The Second Coming. Nothing short of The Blessed Redeemer breaking through the clouds and the roof of that funeral home was to stop the hysterics that were about to hit the front row, the family devastated by loss just a few short moments ago.

"What did you say?"

Aunt Madge got in on it.

"She said she wants to know if you got the flowers."

"Yes."

"Where are they?"

"At the foot of the casket?"

"Where?"

"AT THE FOOT OF THE CASKET ON THE FLOOR WITH THE BLUE RIBBON THAT SAYS 'BROTHER'!"

My Uncle Don began to giggle in a high pitched attempt to stifle it, and Aunt Marianna reached for another Kleenex to hide behind. I drew blood on my left leg by digging my fingernails into my own flesh in hopes of hurting so bad I could cry again. I saw my other uncle. He was bad off, too, and then, my own daddy commenced to laughing. Traitor.

"Oh, I see them. They're pretty."

"WHAT?"

"I said, THEY'RE *PRETTY.*"

At this point, the congregation of mourners began to look our way. Up until then, it was only polite not to stare at the crying, grieving family of the deceased, but now we were either entertaining them or pissing them off. Some laughed with us even if they didn't know why. Some looked at us with disgust, but we could take that 'cause we deserved it. What was bad, what was awful, were the ones who didn't know that in our family if you laugh really, really hard, you cry. We were getting a few folks who took to crying for us. They thought we had all gone to pieces at the same time and it was so unbearably sad that we made them cry and that was more than we could stand.

I heard my Aunt Marianna. It was a sound I know all too well as I make it my own self. It is a cross between a dog's chew toy you've just stepped on, and a cry for help, and it's always followed by, "ohmygod."

Gone. We were gone.

My three great-aunts were oblivious to the hilarity of the front row, minus my grandmother who was measuring us all for caskets of our own.

"I think they did a nice job."

"What?"

"A NICE JOB with the FLOWERS."

"Oh, yeah, they sure did."

A few precious moments of silence before we were dealt the devastating blow.

"How much do I owe you?"

"What?"

"How much do I OWE for the flowers?"

"Oh, twenty-five dollars."

And then, my blessed Aunt Marvel, the woman who just ten minutes before had wailed over her poor, dead brother, screeched in disbelief ...

"TWENTY-FIVE DOLLARS!"

They went to fighting as only sisters can.

"Fine. Just forget it. Don't pay me a dime."

"Oh, I'm gonna pay ye, alright."

"No, just don't pay me. I'll pay for all of them myself."

"Oh no, you won't."

Aunt Marvel bent to the floor and picked up her purse. She paid my Aunt Blanche for the funeral bouquet for their last brother at his service. Some things must be taken care of before you can pray the dead into the sky—everybody knows that is so.

I wrote about Aunt Marvel in the first story I had published. It was a quick mention, but I'm proud that I did it. I don't smoke but I cuss like a sailor, like my Aunt Marvel, and I think she would like that. I still have the books she mailed to me. They were spared in the fire by being in a plastic tub in the barn. Not many, mind you, but I am grateful for them. I think she would like it that I get paid to write stories. I think she would blow smoke into the air, and since she knew I liked books and therefore mailed them to me, she would claim all the credit.

All the damn credit.

BIRDS OF A FEATHER

We refer to our end of town as "The Farms."

Tim Yount has a nice orchard of apple trees. Gantt Sigmon has more chickens than he can keep cooped up. Five of them got took in a failed attempt to release them in the back yard of the high school football coach with a forged "Merry Christmas" note. I know because that plot was hatched in my living room and thwarted by the Claremont police, who caught my boy and five of his best friends and were still laughing about it in the station house a week later.

Truth is, I was the forger.

Gaye Morrison is, without question, the best gardener in town. She can grow it ornamental or edible. Her garden includes everything from blueberries to potatoes to peas and carrots. She's given me good advice, design ideas, fresh lettuce, strawberry pie, bags of bulbs, starts of black-eyed Susan vine and Russian sage, more strawberry pies, fresh cut gladiolas which we both agree are underappreciated, old Mason jars, parts of wooden chairs with tooled leather seats, and a drawing of pumpkins she did in the eighth grade. She is the best neighbor in the entire world, and I will throw rocks at anybody who says otherwise.

I keep trying. I can grow stuff pretty good but am a long way from my goal of making my own goat cheese. I reckon I need goats for that, but I grow what I grow without chemicals, which makes me feel like a farmer and helps make cleaning a horse stall a little more valuable on a seventeen degree morning.

On the other side of Gaye's, on Britt's place, there are all kinds of critters. He has chickens and a big, dumb Saint Bernard and cattle. He used to have a horse but it died. The thing that makes his farm most notable is that Britt is the proud owner of an emu, or as Gaye's husband, the former mayor of this town, refers to him, an "emule."

The emule is hard to miss.

He walks around the pasture closest to the road. Folks new to town, those who don't know any better, slow down to look at him and say, "aww," but not us, not the fine people of Claremont. We keep a safe distance. It's not that the emu is mean or unfriendly. In fact, it's the exact opposite.

Like so many of us in this crazy, mixed up world, the emu falls in love way too easily.

He has been smitten with an Angus bull, a fence post, and a boy who works for the city who still can't talk about it. The emu has romanced trees, a discarded door, a discarded car hood, a discarded horse feeder, and a discarded Big Mac box that someone threw out of the window of their car not knowing that littering was the least of their crimes.

They were, by virtue of that act, accessories to rape.

Two summers ago, my son's pretty little cheerleader girlfriend saw the emu from my back pasture. She couldn't believe her eyes and asked if we could walk across Gaye's property to see him. I thought as long as we stayed on the other side of the fence we'd be fine. The closer we got, though, the more he started to dance and the more I started to worry. Not the cheerleader. She thought he was being cute. It takes awhile to grow out of that, I reckon. It takes some learning to recognize the difference between darling and dangerous behavior and it takes a lifetime to learn when to run.

Gaye stopped digging in her garden to join us as the emu worked himself into a frenzy. I put my arm in front of the cheerleader the same way my grandmother used to throw hers across me when she slammed on the brakes of the Buick, believing that her protection was better than any seat belt Detroit could manufacture. "This is enough," I said. "Best not get any closer."

The emu started this kind of mating ritual that was a cross between a rain dance and the first three seconds after a football is snapped to the quarterback. He hopped from one foot to the other and slammed himself against the fence about ten times before backing up and sort of...crouching. When he did, he proudly displayed all of his manhood.

The cheerleader asked, "Is...is that...is that his...?"

"It really is," I answered.

Gaye goes through life only paying attention to what interests her, and his behavior did not. She chatted on and on while the cheerleader stood frozen and horrified, and I looked for a break in Gaye's monologue to get away from all that the emu was offering. Just when I thought we could make a break for it, Gaye said, "His name is Woody."

He got out one day last spring. I'm a farm girl, born and raised. I've chased a little bit of everything back into a fence that was supposed to hold it. Each species is different. Pigs will oblige you into a false sense of security, then turn and run, squealing all the way. Cattle will give you a clue if you watch them closely, and if you're good at it, you can head them off. I got good at it. I had no idea how to corral an escaped emu, especially one who might make me another notch on his emu headboard.

I saw him from the window of my mudroom and pulled on my muck boots. As I stepped off the porch, wishing like hell I knew Britt's phone number, I saw the mayor come out of his garage.

"The emule is out," he yelled.

He got the job of Mayor in a write-in campaign organized at the Claremont Café when the man who had held that office for years left his wife for a much younger woman, a Yankee, and there wasn't nobody gonna let that slide. Boonie Miller walked up and down the sidewalk in front of the polling place, where in Claremont there was no such thing as a separation of church and state in the basement of the First Baptist Church. Boonie stayed there all day wearing a sandwich board sign that said, front and back, "Vote Glenn Morrison for Mayor. Write it down."

Glenn didn't asked to be our mayor but we have a library in town because of that man. He worked for years and filled out enough paper-work to burn a wet mule, sold Miss Peggy's pound cakes at bake sales, and took tickets for the Merry-Go-Round on Claremont Day because he believed that not having a library defined us as people who didn't want one, and that is not who we are.

I suppose they thought it was sweet, the way he kept coming back to the county offices, the forms they asked for filled out in his own handwriting because never in his life did he believe that a task was beneath him. I'll bet they thought it was cute or dear or some other word that sounds like a compliment but isn't, that he never got irritated when no matter how closely he followed their instructions, he always seemed to get something wrong, something real important in begging for books. I wonder if they felt bad for him when they told him, our Mayor, that he sure had done a fine job getting everything just right, and now all he had to do was to raise ten thousand dollars, and agree to pay half the salary for a librarian in a town where most all the citizens had lost their jobs when three mills closed down, taking their furniture making business to China. I never bothered to count the "For Sale by Bank Foreclosure" signs he must have driven by on his way back to our city limits, where people have farmed a few acres and sewn sofa cushions for at least four generations.

The Mayor asked Miss Peggy to keep baking those pound cakes, and he stood for hours taking tickets from children for a ride on horses made of paint and fiberglass that just went around and around and never got anywhere other than where they'd already been. Tim Yount, the guy with the orchard who makes Apple Pie Moonshine in his kitchen sink, got his real estate license and gave the Mayor the $5,000 commission he made from the sale of one of those foreclosed upon houses; and Gaye used flowers from her garden to decorate the tables for the dinner we hosted when a Southern writer came to town.

People who could not afford it paid $20 for a ticket to hear him read about a brother who could fish real good, and a momma who missed meals so that her boys could eat, and of a grandfather who made and sold 'shine, and buck-danced under Alabama stars.

My people knew all about those kinds of stories.

And, because that Alabama Writer Boy had won a big prize for his stories, lots and lots of folks from other places bought tickets. People who could afford it came to get his name signed in the books they didn't have to beg anybody for.

We got our library.

That Mayor—his daughter graduated from Harvard and his son got a PhD from the college we call "State." I don't suppose it hurts anything for him to mispronounce the name of a nonindigenous species of flightless bird.

THE SPEED OF THE
SOUND OF LONELINESS

I was watching people.

There were twelve or so, maybe more. If you weren't paying good attention, you might think they had all come in together. They were taking up more than half of one end of the bar, talking to each other, dancing with each other. I was alone, on the other side of the room with a notebook and a cell phone.

I could feel the hard seat of the chair I sat in through the hole in the Naugahyde, and the foam that edged out of the wound no one had bothered to recover or repair. It wasn't the kind of place that catered to things like chair cushions or comfort. Those who come there do so either to listen to music or to drink. That's what they'd tell you anyway if you asked. Mostly, I think they come to avoid the sound of loneliness and being empty, and that is an altogether different thing than wanting a drink, though it can be reason enough to want to need one.

It is the beginning of January and it's cold, cold enough to pull the fleece-lined coat from the closet, the wool scarf from the drawer. There was a woman there in a halter top and sandals. Her skirt was so short it barely qualified as a garment. I've seen shop rags with more cloth. She was twenty-five pounds too heavy for either of the wardrobe pieces she was wearing, even if it had been July. If she'd been picking up a carton of smokes and a box of Moon Pies, she'd have ended up in one of them People of Walmart emails folks find funny and forward on to their friends.

Her hair was dyed more of a maroon than a true red and cut in a spiky short style, her earrings big and loopy and cheap. That halter was undeserving of the trust she put in it when she danced, alone and bouncing, in one corner of the dance floor. It was under quite a strain to keep things where she'd put them. I saw her adjust the important stuff more than once. I guessed her to be fifty-five. She's lived a lot more than that though.

Another woman, also dancing alone, always dancing alone, was frighteningly thin. Her eyes were hollow, her hair dead from all that she does to keep it bleached blonde and big. She's always there. She doesn't stick to one corner but travels along the edge of the floor by herself, eyes closed mostly until she needs to make the corner in a sort of sharp turn, spinning once, and taking one step backward before turning and moving on down the next side. She wants it to appear as though she is lost in the music. I think she is just lost.

A third woman fakes a British accent. I ran into her in the ladies room. She told me she was in show business. Had been her whole life, she said.

I reckon so.

I've spent a lot of time in the past two years, sitting in a chair in my own bedroom. I write there. I eat there. I watch *Law and Order* and *House* there. With Walker gone to college, there is very little of the house that gets used except when he is home, and with him come forty-seven others, consuming groceries and arguing over the best color of blue uniform. When they leave, it seems quieter than it was before they came.

I think that is the sound those women in that bar are trying not to hear.

It would be easy to make fun of them. I have better taste in clothes and the good fortune to have been able to support my taste by calling up some nice customer service representative and then waiting for that brown truck to roll in with the coat everyone compliments, or the boots no one else has.

Not even Shelley Setzer.

I have that sweet little cupcake of a hair do-er, Ashton, and therefore, unless the humidity's high and the flat iron's broke, I have good
hair. People tell me they like it. Men tell me they like it. I am neither
too thin nor too fat and my accent, while stronger in some circles, I will
grant you, ain't British, but it is mine. It would be easy to laugh at these
women, to see them as clichés, to dismiss them as barflies, and believe
we have nothing in common.

But lonely, turns out, ain't that particular as to hair and wardrobe and
it doesn't give a damn about your taste. It will come and get you when it
wants you, in a room by yourself, or in a crowd of people or with a man
lying on the other side of a too small bed that's far too big.

Sometimes it creeps up on you and you never see it coming, though
all your friends will tell you that they did. Sometimes it hits hard and
quick and you're neck deep into a lake of trouble before you realize why
you signed up for the cruise, and you hear Henley singing, faint and
soft, "Oh my god, I can't believe it's happening again."

Sometimes it isn't the company of others you're missing at all. Sometimes it's the best of you that gets gone, and despite all your efforts you
can't find that person you're most proud of being, and that right there is
the worst: being lonely for you.

I'm a writer. I'm a mother. I'm a cook. I'm a Lovie. I'm a good dancer.
I can sing better than most folks know. I can see through the walls that
people build either to hide or protect themselves, and more often than
not, I can get through them. I can break through, chip at the mortar, kick
at the brick until I have reached the ones others, long ago, gave up on
with good reason. I am proud of that.

I am ashamed when I don't try.

I can understand the meaning in song lyrics, can commit them to
memory more than most musicians. They hate me for that. I can recite
most of "The Walrus and the Carpenter," and when asked recently how
old I was when I learned, my answer was the truth. I didn't learn it, not
really. I just read it.

Some things stick.

I have been lonely for weeks, telling people I was, emailing friends,
sending messages of "I sure do miss you," and looking for new friendships
and new people with walls to break through; spending far too much
time on social media, depending on witty remarks, mostly my own, for

entertainment and distraction. It's been coming to me slowly.

I miss me.

I miss who I like to be when I can, when it seems to take no effort to try. I miss the way I see and navigate the world. I miss drinking from a glass half full. I miss putting others first. I miss my gratitude, my appreciation for the little things others miss. I miss being the one to point them out to the beauty-blind or the deaf or the stone dumb, and the feeling that comes from knowing I am the one who brought them along. I miss being good. I miss being happy. I miss the smile on a face when I walk into a room. I miss *the me* that inspired such a smile.

I miss my best writing voice. I haven't heard it in a long, long time.

I listened as women near me, in that bar, made fun of those others. I heard what they said. It must be easy to live in that world where you have no real self-scrutiny, no trouble believing you are superior to others who buy their hair color down at the Kmart and don't seem to own a mirror. I don't live with that ease. I see myself in almost every face. I wonder what it would be like to be them, be him, be her, and I wonder if I am, if I am that lonely, only in better clothes. I wonder what small moment of grace keeps me from dancing around the edges of a floor under a mirrored ball, needing folks to look at me but pretending I don't, or pulling a tube top over my ass and calling it a skirt, and going to the parking lot with a man who, an hour ago, didn't know my name.

The answer comes back, not that much, not that much difference at all.

There is a big difference in me and the women who point and laugh and say that the five dollar cover was the best money they ever paid for such entertainment. At least, I hope so. I watched them for a long time, listened to their conversation, which never had any redeeming value but only served to tear down the others in the meanest way possible. I reckon when *Mockin'bird* was assigned in their English class, they thought it was enough to pass the test. Me, I learned to walk around in another man's skin, at least to try.

I don't think their skin would fit me. It's miles too thick. Mine is paper-thin and scars real easy.

One of my best friends is in the middle of an ocean. Five are half a country away. One is on the far end of the other half and has been for too long. Two of them are in Alabama. I am my best self when they are around, when they are daily reminders of the way I want to be, the music

I want to hear, the words I want to write. I miss them, the friends, the songs, and the words I can't get to come just right, the words that drown out the sound of loneliness.

I miss the good me.

UNCONDITIONAL

I used to know a man in Frankfurt, Germany who shipped all kinds of exotic things. He had pictures of interesting stuff folks had asked him to get from point A to point B tacked to a bulletin board in his office in the cargo section of the Frankfurt airport. He spoke at least three languages fluently, often at the same time, juggling phone calls with givers and getters, and I loved him so. He referred to me as "sweet," which ain't a bit true, but he did it so regular that another German with less affinity for the inefficient American way of having fifty words that mean the same thing, called me.

"Hey, I talk to Jo Wanner and he luffs you."

"I love him, too."

"Yah, okay, listen to dis. He says, 'I *luff* dis girl. She is sweet.' What is dis word? What is 'sweet'?"

Explaining Jo's use of the word to a typical German national is not so easy. The stereotype that with Germans everything is black or white is not really accurate. It is that things are either the darkest depth of nothing or all sunshine and light. No middle ground. There is no opinion, only fact. All questions can be explained with logic and clear thinking. There is no wonderment or mysticism, nothing unexplainable or unexplained.

Except dogs.

They adhere to the strictest of breeding practices and time-honored training methods, sure, but you can get the toughest hard-ass German to the point of wiping tears if you ask him about his favorite dog. He will look to the sky and shake his head and say, "He was special. I don't know why but, dis is truth."

I know folks who believe that all dogs are special but that isn't so. It isn't on account of being kicked real hard or ignored or starved or left in the back yard on a chain. Some are just regular dogs. That alone is better than most people, but the special ones, the ones you get if you are lucky, are impossible to get over once they're gone. It ought to be that way. It should be painful. Otherwise we'd get all confused and think that running off to the neighbor with the unexpected litter of twelve, and toting home a critter that will eat the legs off your couch and pee on the T-shirt you threw on the floor, will make up for the loss.

It never has, and as far as I can tell, it never will.

One of the special ones was lost last week. There are pictures of them, a baby boy and the dog he didn't know wasn't his, that might would scare people who don't know any better. She was bigger than most good-sized ponies and his tiny hands grabbing a fist full of dog jowls could have caused a lesser dog, or even a regular one, to snap in self-defense. Not Samantha. She licked him, and Jack, in total trust, only closed his eyes but did not pull away from the giant head with the giant mouth full of giant teeth.

His trust was in her giant heart.

I feel cheated that I did not know this dog, but I loved her; and her loss, though not as profound to me as to those who spent their days with her, is painful and as big as she was. Through photographs, I saw her allow my sweet Jack to sit on her and under her. I saw her let him keep the cracker in his dimpled hand that she could have easily taken from him. I watched her tolerate the pinching hugs, the running tackles, the accidental kicks of tiny tennis shoes without so much as a whimper—and she was only a year and half of another.

That is special.

On a recent road trip I packed a photograph of Walker, one of Matilda and Jack, and one of Paja, the dog I will never replace and though ten years have passed since she did, I still mourn. I packed a picture of Nate and Abbie taken at Big Bear with the dog that, even mentioned in conversation, will bring floods of tears from my oldest child, nearly thirty-two years old. That dog was so in love with her that when his arthritic joints ached too much to follow her up the stairs, he would sit at the bottom and wait, staring up for what to him was an eternity, but according to the clock couldn't have been more than a minute or two.

When she brought Matilda home from the hospital and sat propped up on pillows in her bed, me rocking the baby in the corner of the room, Fran, a black German Shepherd dog, checked first his Abbie, then his new baby in my arms, and walked back to the door, circled twice, and slumped to the floor. He sighed with his whole body and Abbie and I laughed. Finally, he had all his girls in one room. We weren't getting out and nobody was getting in. Two months later, Abbie propped Matilda up against his side to take their picture. He circled his body around her, as obsessed with her as he was her momma, Matilda looking tiny and somewhat annoyed by his constant hovering.

Ain't that always the way? We don't want the attention if boys are too free to give it.

It wasn't much later that he was gone. I had told Nate on that last visit to get ready, to be ready to hold Abbie up and together, and I told Walker we should say a real goodbye. We wouldn't see him again.

Walker taught him to play basketball. He would wait for the shot, wait for the command, but when Walker said, "Fran, bring!" he would run so hard to get and retrieve the smaller ball Walker used just for him, he would hit the back fence head on. Didn't phase him. He knew how to play a version of football, chasing Walker until he tagged him, then happily running the other way, and would "go out for a pass" like his name was Jerry Rice and catching the Nerf football meant a Super Bowl Ring and a trip to Disneyland. He ran with Abbie on the streets of San Diego as she trained for mini-marathons, did perfect obedience, according to them hard-ass Germans, and knew when to bite and when to let go. They say he should have been the World Champion, his talent and his willingness to do as he was asked unmatched. But he had his trophy. He had his Abbie and he died a happy dog knowing, somehow, a smaller version of her had shown up, so there was another to love.

He was special.

I had a story published about Kate, the dog that was supposed to help me get over Paja, but took to Walker instead. The only time she chose to stay with me was when I had pneumonia and could only sleep sitting up. She was old and hurting by that time, but when I had run out of Kleenex and took the extra toilet paper for wiping my nose, she got up, pulled herself to her feet when I dropped it and it rolled across the floor. That sweet old dog, as she had done with freezers full of ducks, fetched that roll of paper and brought it to me so I did not have to get out of my chair. I cried my stuffed-up head off. She just laid back down and went to snorin'.

Special.

Paja told me that Walker was to come down with the chicken pox. She did so, and I have witnesses. She was a highly trained German Shepherd, but the only person she ever bit was a man I should have shot dead. No jury would have convicted either one of us. Another time, she jumped in the front seat of my Expedition and barked in my face until I got back in the car, which annoyed me to no end until I learned, a week later, that the building I was parked in front of was broken into and robbed at the exact time I was there. She stopped Walker from leaving the yard by blocking his path until he got tired and quit trying, though that is not a part of any training she had. If there was a baby in the house, any baby, she would pace until the momma gave the baby to me. Then she would lie down at my feet, satisfied that all was right with the world. Had I asked her to, she would have knitted me a sweater.

She was that special.

And now we have lost another, Jack's big buddy, Sammy. They say it is the unconditional love we crave and they so freely give that makes us love dogs. I reckon so. Still, any dog can do that or most can, anyway. Paja and Fran and Kate and Samantha had that magic, that unknown ingredient in the batter. If we could breed it, we damn sure would. If we could be it, we damn sure should, but it doesn't have a name. There is no word for it either in German, or English, which has a dozen words for love.

I know this: our family has had its share of the dogs everyone who truly loves them wishes for. It scares me to pieces that we won't get another, that our allotment is all used up, that whoever is keeping score is hip to the fact that we are well over our quota.

But if that's so, I am grateful that Jack had his Sammy before they stopped handing us the special ones. He will remember her. I believe that. The children who loved her will grow up to tell their children about the daycare dog and everyone will think they are exaggerating her size. They will see a tiny dog and remember her. They will see a big dog and remember her. If they forget her name along the way, they will not forget her heart and how safe they felt in her presence, how drowned they felt when she licked them, how much fun it was to see the grownups gasp when they first saw her.

I will remember those baby hands.

I will remember the look in Samantha's eye as Jack squeezed tight, no matter how many times his momma said, "Gentle, gentle," and how anybody who knows anything could have looked at that dog and known who she was.

She was special.

A WRITER,
TWO DOG KENNELS,
A DALE JR. CUTOUT,
AND A LESBIAN

It's been a rough week.

I've been tuning out most people who took a notion to talk to me. For reasons that defy explanation, neither my well-documented independence nor fear for their lives has kept almost everyone I know from starting their sentences with, "What you need to do is..."

I love advice like that. It assumes that the person receiving it lacks the ability to reason or think without the influence and assistance of the advice giver. I reckon it is steadfast security in their superiority that makes them so confident when they throw their heads back and begin with, "What you need to do is..."

Last night, in the parking lot of the Conover Tavern, Roxanne Moser sucked in the smoke of a quick cigarette, blew it back into the frozen air and said, "What you *need* to do, Shari, is to say, 'What *you* need to do is kiss my ass.'"

She's the only one who's been right.

I woke this morning to the third day of critter sounds in the walls. I've heard it all. What you need to do is...(1) Poison them. I suppose that requires the least amount of actual help from the advice giver. I considered it when I realized that my house would smell so bad from the carcasses rotting in the walls most of these folks would stay away for a while. (2) Call an exterminator. No one with ovaries gave me this advice. If there is one industry worse at being honest with women than used car salesmen, it's a man who is talking to you while you're standing on a chair, shrieking. He knows you'll pay. Oh, he knows. (3) Climb up on an extension ladder to the highest peak of your two-story hundred year old farmhouse and nail chicken wire/hardware cloth/a piece of tin/a notice of eviction over the hole you aren't really sure is there. If I had an extension ladder that would reach that high, I'm pretty sure I shouldn't be on it, and I'm damn sure I should be holding nails in my teeth, or whacking them with a hammer.

I have a hard time asking for help. This week has not inspired me to alter that. But, like I knew he would, when I asked the mayor, he came as soon as Gaye told him to.

He came into the hallway and listened. "You have squirrels in your walls. What you need to do is get them out."

Before he went home, he was in the attic, in the other attic, under the house, on the house, and in the end said, "What you need to do is poison them."

At least he showed up.

Trayci Allen walked through the back door wearing a black T-shirt over long underwear, a pair of cargo shorts, and a baseball cap. She apologized for her tardiness but she'd been under a car all morning. She was in the attic, in the other attic, under the house, and on the house. She sat quietly in the living room for ten minutes and then spoke.

"I figured it out. What you needed to do was call a lesbian first."

The squirrel, not squirrels, was not trying to avail himself of my hospitality, but in fact was trapped. When I finally got quiet enough to listen I realized she was right. Trayci wanted to save him, to help him in his hour of need. I wanted him not to die in the space between my office and a guest bedroom.

We came up with a plan.

When this house was renovated, long before I bought it, their goal was to rip every shred of character and personality out of it and cover it in fake everything. Laminate floors instead of hardwood, drywall instead of beadboard, and, the bane of my existence, two white Roman columns that marked the dreaded wallboard from the only thing they didn't rip out and burn, the knotty pine in the living room. I hated those columns, loathed them, daydreamed about the day they were gone, gone, gone and even pitching a good fit wouldn't bring them back.

Turns out, that day was today.

Trayci reasoned that if we took one of the columns off we were going to discover a big enough separation that the squirrel could get out and be free as he was born to be. I did not think that he needed to be free anywhere near my 42 inch flat screen television. Ah, yes, this was a problem, she agreed. If he gets out, how will we get him out of the house?

As we sat together trying to figure out how, the squirrel ran above our heads from one wall to the other, stopping occasionally to chew or to cry a little. Trayci said, "Poor baby."

My ass.

Eureka! She had it. We needed plywood and lots of it. We could build a sort of chute, much like for cattle, where he would emerge from the hole in the wall, run into the chute that in her mind looked like something that would inspire the admiration of the boys on *This Old House*, and run to the open front door. Trayci sent me to the barn for every piece of scrap plywood I could find, a hammer, some nails, and a tarp if I could find one.

A tarp wasn't the only thing I couldn't find.

I had to improvise. I searched through all the glorious, wondrous things that live in the loft of my barn, waiting, waiting for the day they are put to good use.

Turns out, that day was today.

I barely made it to the house, but in one trip I brought Trayci everything she would need to build her masterpiece. I came through the door with an old window, the sides of two dog kennels, and a giant cardboard cutout of Dale Earnhardt Jr.

She stared at me like bats were flying out of my ears.

This would work. I was sure of it. I showed her that Junior's cutout actually folded out to make *two* of NASCAR's favorite driver. I linked the sides of the kennel until they stretched across the hallway and to the door. We lined it all up, right to the hole Trayci uncovered by removing the horrible white column, turned off the lights so as not to scare him, and waited for him to trot happily out to his tree house where he would live the rest of his days haunted by the claustrophobic memory of being caught in a sea of insulation, vowing and insisting his little squirrel friends swear the same oath, to never again attempt to break into my house. Trayci collapsed into a chair and repeated that I should have called a lesbian and never turned over such a delicate operation to a man. I took the couch. We stared at the hole.

Nothing.

"I've been in the dark with women before," Trayci said, "but never doing this." We laughed and then hushed each other again, turning our attention to the hole in the wall.

Nothing.

"I think we need a light," I said to Trayci. "Something that he can see from inside the wall and know there is a way out." She turned on the lamp beside her chair.

Nothing.

"Do you think we need more light or less light?" she asked. More, I reasoned, and she turned on another table lamp. She reached for and flipped on the overhead light and I snapped, "Too much. Trayci, that is too much light."

Offended, she turned around and said, "Dammit, Shari, I've never done this before. It's my first time."

I said, "Isn't that usually the line you hear from girls like me?"

She turned off the overhead light, sat back down, and we waited.

Nothing.

My phone buzzed, the sound of a text message. A friend wanted to know what I was doing, so I told him. It was like Marlon Perkins and Jim Fowler in drag. Well, sort of in drag. Trayci's fairly butch, but my mascara was perfection and it had been a good hair day.

He laughed too hard to text back right away, but he's a good lookin', fast ridin' cowboy and so wrote, "Should I bring my rope?" I read it to Trayci who thought that was a great idea.

I'm reasonably certain she meant for the squirrel, but not entirely.

Trayci's girlfriend sent her a text that basically said we were too dumb for our own good, that squirrels sleep at night, and we were in great shape if we needed bait because both of us were nuts.

Trayci decided to wake him up.

She took down the other column I have hated every day in the nearly three years I have lived here, while I watched the exit door. She banged a hammer and popped the wood as she tugged it from the wall, making all kinds of noise. It must have woken him; he stuck his head out, looked around the room, and pulled it back in, terrified I reckon on account of when I yelled, "There he is, Trayci, turn around! He's right there!"

Right up to that moment, Trayci had said that for a woman, I was being remarkably calm.

In the end, she nailed pieces of tin leftover from my self installed backsplash, with Plan B being that we would try again in the morning. Trayci went home to Sherrie, who was frying hamburgers, and I locked myself and the dogs in my bedroom, hoping he wasn't a third shift squirrel, ready after just a few hours sleep to go to work chewing my cable wire in two. The chute, made of an old window, a toy box, a birdhouse, an old chair, a new chair, two dog kennels, and a Dale Junior cutout sits at the ready, the work of art that it is, waiting to make history.

And before anyone says it, I know, I know...next time, what I *need* to do is call a lesbian. What I need to do is call a good friend.

What I need to do, is call Trayci.

GET BUSY

I don't remember the first time I saw her. She was there until she wasn't.

I have memories of piling in the back of her family station wagon on the way to pick out a golden retriever puppy they named Rex, of hearing her father call, "Come on, little goats!" and, on cue, yelling in unison with her brothers, "We're not goats! We're KIDS!"

"I always get that wrong," he would say, grinning to let us know he wasn't a bit confused. I remember a mean pony named Moe and the girl we convinced to take a ride, identical dolls for Christmas when we were seven and eight, identical birthstone rings when we were twelve and thirteen, and playing a 45 of "American Pie" four thousand times until both of us had memorized it to perfection.

She was all the things I wasn't.

At sixteen, she was prettier than I would ever be. She was an "it girl" before there was such a thing. I was an "if only." She was perfectly proportioned where I was too much or too little. Her hair would curl if she brushed it just so or lay stick straight and smooth, while I would have to wait years on the availability of a flat iron to make mine behave.

If other girls were jealous, I was not.

I needed her too much.

Carey Simmons would talk me into crawling through the open window of our church basement to have several sips of communion wine. No one can squeeze the good out of anything quite like generic, milquetoast, fence-riding Christians, so it wasn't really wine but rather grape juice, but it felt for all the world like unbridled sin. It would be years before I knew what unbridled sin actually was, and that it was a whole hell of a lot better than grape juice in a church basement. I remember being shocked that lightning didn't strike us dead, and looking at the tiny glass cup that had held the power of the Blood without realizing that someone had poured it out of a carton they bought at the grocery store, and put the rest in the Frigidaire. Carey knew, though. I could tell by the look on her face. "Oh, go on. It's just grape juice," she shrugged, as she took another swig.

She would sit on the edge of my bed, trying to convince me that I did not have to take the abuse of people who were supposed to love me, but she would be gone before I would put that into practice. She was right. Bullies come in all shapes and titles, and if you grab their hair a quick second after they've taken hold of yours, they back on down. Carey knew that there was no more real power there than there had been in those little glass cups. She walked through life knowing things like that. I was just happy to be walking in her footsteps, to spend my high school years as "that girl with Carey."

That would change with one phone call. The buffer I thought I needed would vanish in the middle of the night with no more warning than a wave out a football player's car window leaving Carter's parking lot.

I answered before I was awake. Mark Morris would tell me to sit up, to wake up and sit up, that he had bad news. "Carey is dead," he said,, and I told him to shut up, that it wasn't funny. He said he knew that. Then I believed him.

Mark and his brother Rick had come along the scene, the eighteen-wheeler that hit a teenager's car broadside, passenger side, taking Carey instantly, and her quarterback boyfriend fifteen minutes later. It had taken Rick and Mark more than an hour to get their dad to let them call me. I didn't cry. I didn't scream. I pulled on Levis and went to Carey's house.

Her mother would sit quietly in a chair all night while Daddy Jack paced the floor and sobbed. I would end up at Diana Etchison's house, watching her daddy pound on the washing machine because, sometimes, there is no dog to kick. He would call Ted Morris, asked him if it was real or "Did Shari dream it?" Mark's daddy would have the unenviable job of telling Dallas that a child he loved like his own was gone.

She was sixteen years old.

Less than a month before, Carey had played Nellie in our school's production of *South Pacific*. She washed a man out of her hair in a packed gymnasium for three nights as I sat in awe of her onstage kiss and complete confidence. The morning after she died, the same kids who sang and danced with her were on a bus on our way to a regional contest. We were given the opportunity to pass. We got on the bus.

I would be the first to step on the stage. I was in Carey's place. Later, the girl who stood next to me would tell me how brave I was, that she didn't know how I did it. Bravery had nothing to do with it. It was pure numbness and nothing else. I felt nothing. Bravery would belong to someone else that morning. Bravery would be for Jackie.

In an eerie twist, our director had selected a song that pondered questions we were too young to be asking, but on that morning, we knew the answers. We had gotten through the first selection, a song I cannot recall, and the second, "Jesus, Thou Joy." The auditorium was full. Word had spread that we had lost our star the night before and whether it was morbid curiosity or a show of support, all the other schools had come in to listen to us.

Truth was, we were terrified of Mrs. Reveal. She didn't weigh ninety pounds soaking wet, but she was a tyrant. We breathed in the right rests, hit the right notes, pronounced words we didn't understand exactly as she wanted us to, and she had no problem humiliating any one of us if we didn't.

Except Carey.

If we were lost on that morning, Mrs. Reveal was no less so. She adored her Nellie. We all knew she had selected *South Pacific* because Carey was perfect for the role. She had told us, with uncharacteristic kindness, that we needed to hold ourselves together, to get through these three songs—but we knew it wasn't a request. Devastated or not, we feared the wrath of Wreatha Reveal.

It was the very thing Carey had tried to teach me, that some things are more powerful than fear.

I can see her still, Jackie Henry, in the middle of the choir and the risers. She had been Bloody Mary to Carey's Nellie. She had "Happy Talked" and delivered the signature "Bali Hai" song only twenty days earlier like a pro.

In the last lines of our last song, our high school choir—kids grief stricken, broken hearted—sang, *"Did I ever love? Did I ever give? Did I ever really live?"*

Jackie Henry was the only one of us, the only one, to do what we all should have done. She sobbed. She allowed herself to feel it, all of it, the loss, the grief, the fury, the pain, and she cried in front of an audience who rose to their feet and clapped. She wasn't concerned about reprimands or contest placement. She was real and in so, she was brave.

Jackie runs the local paper, now. I think that's perfect. We need newspaper editors who will allow themselves to feel. I'm glad it's Jackie.

I learned many things from Carey Simmons, both in her life and after her death. I would remain tied to her through her older brother and Special Olympics. Mike used to make me laugh. Carey taught me it was okay to do that, to laugh. "He's funny," she'd say. "If I did what he did, you'd laugh, so laugh when he does it." I took him to see *E.T.* at the Diana Theater. In the middle of the movie, Mike loudly asked me, "Why don't they just give him the telephone?"

Good question.

I would go see her parents while they still lived in the home place. One time we watched a home movie of the dress rehearsal of *South Pacific*. We all cried but we laughed when Carey mugged for the camera. "Same ol' Carey," her mother would say, as if time could still change her, as if she wasn't going to be beautiful and sixteen forever in our memories.

When my baby, Abbie, was born, Jack and Carol came to see her and brought her a red and white gingham checked dress. I had her six-month picture taken in it. Carol rocked her and cried. When my grandmother died, we stood together in the same funeral home where we'd stood years before and talked about the remake of *South Pacific*. Carol said she knew I had watched it.

In the days after Carey died, people would say that everything happens for a reason. I looked for that reason for a long time, for years. I never found it. Instead, I came to believe that things happen because things happen, and that it is up to us to make something out of them, to learn something. I do not believe, not for one minute, that there was some greater good in the deaths of two teenagers, that there was divine guidance in the grief that their mothers would suffer for the rest of their lives.

Last winter, more than thirty years later, I went to the nursing home to see Carol Simmons. Carey was her mother's daughter. Carol's hair was perfectly done as was her manicure, and she was wearing lipstick. She seemed to recognize me the minute I came through the door but was crying before I could hug her and never stopped through my entire visit. Without really looking at me, she would say, "You're so beautiful," over and over. I patted her and said, "Carol, don't cry. We have happy things to remember." She would blow her nose and nod, but then shake her head and say, "You're so beautiful." When she finally met my eyes, when finally she looked at me, she said, "You're not Carey, are you?"

Please do not try and tell me that any sort of god had some great plan on the day Carey Simmons died.

What I did, what I learned from that day, is that we had better get busy. Though it is a source of endless embarrassment to my children, I never let good things go unsaid. I will compliment a stranger on her choice of coat or scarf, tell the boys at the Back Table how very much I need them to be there, morning after morning. I write paragraphs on Margaret Garrison's many virtues and profoundly bad taste in jewelry. I never hang up without telling Debbie Frazier I love her because I do. When my cousin Marqie says something funny, which by the way is often, I tell her and tell my daddy because he thinks she's funny, too.

I've been the butt of many a joke as to my unabashed emotion. Alisa Carpenter has been known to take bets on the exact moment I will start crying when I get up in front of this town, like she's one to talk. I've had folks wave Kleenex in the air to move me a little closer to their bet. There are folks who think me downright unstable because I will hug half the people in The Café before leaving and regularly kiss Jeff Bolick flat on the mouth.

I know this.

There is no one I love who does not know it. There is no one I believe to be smart or funny who hasn't heard me say it or read about my admiration in a magazine. My daddy, as ill as he is, has lived to read stories he thought I had forgotten. He now knows I didn't forget and he knows I won't. If too many people have misunderstood the words "I love you" to mean "I will take an endless amount of shit from you," well, they soon learned that there is a difference. That's not my fault. That's on them.

Carey died knowing how I felt. I wrote it to her in a card I gave her before she took the stage on April 2, 1976. It was the only peace I had for six months after she died, knowing that she knew. Her sister, Caren, told me that she kept the card, put it in a box of things that belonged to Carey.

I learned that you had better say it, better live it, from Carey Simmons. I learned not to be one bit embarrassed about it from Jackie Henry.

And it's about time I thanked her for that.

CAN'T YOU FEEL THE SUNSHINE

My granddaddy was a horseman. He didn't own fine, quick-footed quarter horses or showy Arabians with ribbons in their manes and silver on their saddles. Pa's horses were, like him, working class. He had Belgians and other drafts—mules, too. They didn't ride the trail or keep a calf rope tight. They pulled weight, their own and whatever needed moving. They worked long days in fields turning over dirt for planting crops that would keep a family and other creatures fed over a winter that must have seemed longer than it was.

Born to a family of too many, my granddaddy had little choice but to quit school and leave home at the age of thirteen. He went to work, making his own way. He got a job logging in the hills of Tennessee where his gift would shine. They say he could drive the big Belgians and sure-footed mules dragging the felled lumber from the woods without laying a hand on a line. He needed only his voice. A quiet "gee" or "haw" and a soft and low "whoa, there" was all it took. He had a way, a gentleness they understood, and if anybody confused his ease with weakness they need only have watched him put a ring through a bull's nose. It wasn't weakness. It was understanding. Had he been born in another time or place, folks would have called him a prodigy and written books and magazine articles about him, but he was poor Tennessee hill people and nobody thought about writing down his stories.

He only has me.

He planted strawberries in rows, not in patches like most gardeners. Two long, straight rows ran the length of a flat stretch of land with a pan of water at one end and a pan of scratch corn at the other. Two ducks and an old goose spent the growing season walking from pan to pan, and along the way eating bugs and picking bits of weeds and grass that were coming up between the strawberry plants, eliminating the need for insecticide and doing all Pa's weeding for him. They took care of the fertilizing, too. That makes me laugh out loud. These organic farmers with their own TV shows are just a little late to the party. God knows, he was smart.

He saved ammunition by never shooting a crow, instead boring a hole with his knife in kernels of corn he kept in an old cigar box, threading a single hair from the tail of one of the horses through each piece, and leaving them on a fence post. Crows would swallow the corn and, sparing the ugly details, let's just say there was no need to shoot them. Some will claim it as an act of cruelty, but his fields grew tall with healthy, unharmed crops, and his children stayed fed. I don't mind crows, kinda like them, but then crows are not a threat to my ability to feed my family. I will remember this story as yet another example of how well his thinking served him and how resourceful he could be.

He would stop at his friend's house, an old black man with the same kind of growing up story as my Pa's and sit on the porch to visit. Privilege and power eluded them both and other than the color of their skin, their lives had been the same. Anyone who says that southern country people are racists never spent any time here. I know better.

I come from better.

I have a small piece of his harness, a swivel my daddy gave to me. I have the ring for the nose and a pulley that attached to the chain that made sure no bull jumped the fence for reasons of lust or freedom. I have his tobacco knife and the rope and ring he used to control pigs that forgot whose farm they were born to. Alisa Carpenter put supper on the table for her family and came to help me sift through ashes and charred beams to find them, and wiped them clean to hang in a place of honor in my new-old house, after my old-old house caught fire and burned beyond saving. Not even those flames could keep them from me. If I had given up, Alisa wouldn't have. She ain't made thataway.

In the middle of a kitchen that was left in ruins was the oil lamp my great-grandmother gave to my grandparents when they went to housekeeping. It was unbroken, unharmed. Folded just as I left them, without scorch or tear, were two quilts my grandmother made from the summer dresses of my aunts and my daddy and granddaddy's work shirts. Everything else on those shelves, my books and collection of shiny glass horses, were destroyed, but the quilts were just sitting there like they were waiting on me.

I can't explain it. I just know it's so.

When I was able to accept the loss of a house I loved, and the reality of needing a place to live started to seep in, Alisa nudged me toward a small farm at the edge of town. She said it looked like me. The big, white farm house had five bedrooms and almost as many bathrooms that would need cleaning. Alisa stood in front of the kitchen sink and said that she could just see the whole town gathered there for my annual Christmas party, the one I host on the first Saturday in December after the Claremont Christmas Parade, all three blocks of it. It was the view from those kitchen windows I was most interested in.

There was a barn.

It had a new metal roof, but most of the north side was gone. The original hardware held the remnants of a door with so many rotted boards it looked to be smiling with missing teeth. It was full of hardened bags of concrete, thrown out cabinets, and a rusty bicycle with flat tires; things of no good use to anyone anymore. The track was there, but the hay forks were gone. I ran my hand along the curve of board that showed the wear of a cribbing horse. I nodded to Alisa. She grinned ear to ear and pulled the cell from her pocket. "Hey, this is Alisa. I'm fixin' to write up an offer on that place you got for sale."

In the days after I moved in, the men who sit at the Back Table of our local diner, the Claremont Café, called me muleheaded when I refused to use a fancy sprayer they offered to lend me and chose to dip a brush in a can of red paint, over and over. Alisa's daddy shored up the north side, nailing new boards over hundred-year-old studs, putting in new windows he found on sale, and building me a new barn door with an X brace. I painted the trim and the fence brown despite the daily argument at The Café as to whether I should have chosen black or white. Now that it's done and sunflowers bloom along the south side, a metal horse tank overflows with a pine tree and black-eyed Susans, and I propped up the old beachcomber bicycle behind some milk cans I painted, folks say it looks just like it was supposed to.

I reckon so.

I had a basketball goal installed so my boy and his buddies could play through the winter. Their parents know to look here first when their young'uns go missing for too long. Once they were taken care of, I got in my truck and drove down J.B. Road to the Bumgarner sawmill. I thought of Jerry.

He wore bib overalls and sported a killer Fu Manchu mustache and would call to me when I came in The Café for breakfast. "Lookee here, boys. There she comes, the prettiest smart girl in town," which was my cue to feign serious offense and demand that he tell me who it was, who was the dumb girl better looking than me. It was our greeting. He died one early spring night, six feet from his own driveway, when he couldn't miss the deer running from the pine woods. They told me and Alisa early the next day when we went to the volunteer fire department's pancake breakfast. They separated us first. Even brave firefighters know better than to take on two squalling women at the same time.

I miss Jerry. I miss him bad.

So does Rick, his little brother, who runs the mill during the day, and deejays down at the White Pine on Thursday nights. He gave me a better deal on rough cut lumber than he should have and delivered it for nothing. Their nephew, Mike, who calls me "ma'am" 'cause he's supposed to, dropped it off right in front of the barn and said he'd thrown a few extra boards on the truck, and that he'd cut more if I needed it.

I can hear the pounding and the whir of the power saws coming from the barn. They are building me a stall, making it strong and pretty because I do like pretty, and can get tiresome to working men trying to do their job and get home for supper. It's a big stall because my horse won't be quick or showy either. That wouldn't do.

Her name is Sunshine. When she is grazing, I will see her from the kitchen and from the window at this desk. When she is working she will give rides to Claremont children and visitors wanting to look at Christmas lights. We won't charge much and we'll give the money to the library. I cannot wait to get Miss Maybell and Miss Glenna May in the back of that carriage and ride them around.

Crazy old women.

Matilda will brush her, as Sunshine stands dead still. She has been a momma. She's a momma kind of horse and will know to step lightly around our baby girl. On early morning rides I will tell Matilda that her great-great-grandfather had horses just like Sunshine, that he plowed fields for crops and hauled logs to build houses for people. I will tell her of the strawberries and the old goose and two ducks and show her the tools he used to make a life for the family that came before her, before her mother, before me. The connection between my granddaddy and working Belgian horses will go on to its fifth generation, a little girl named Matilda with big, brown eyes he would have loved, and had he known her, would have asked to come on over and give him some sugar. He would have also told her not to let the dog lick her in the face, but she wouldn't have paid a bit more attention to that than I did.

When I can, I will tell her of the house that burned, the house I loved. I will tell her that it had a porch that wrapped all the way around and wide plank floors, but not nearly enough land for us to make trails or feed deer. I will speak of the fancy carving in the fireplace mantel in the front room where they tell me Goober Green, the town drunk for a time, (who liked to sing, "I'm Goober Green from New Orleans, I ain't been sober since last October") lay in his coffin while his momma received pound cake and sympathy from Claremont mourners.

I will tell Matilda that I pulled the drywall from every room and found beadboard and wainscoting and another three feet of ceiling, but there was no barn to restore, no place to build a stall. There was no farm. I will tell her that sometimes the very things that bring us to our knees turn out to be what we needed most, that I could only have china horses to set on shelves in that house. In that house, there could be no Sunshine.

I will tell her that story when it doesn't hurt me anymore.

When I look at that horse, in my mind, I will hear James Taylor sing of this Carolina, *"Can't you see the Sunshine, can't you just feel the moonshine?"* and hope that, though I am one state east of where my granddaddy might like me to be, that he knows I am with good people, that I am doing my best to take care of his story and wishing I had paid more attention when he had lessons to teach. A horse named Sunshine will carry me through the foothills of Catawba County and I will hear my Pa say, "Tell dogs what to do, but ask horses for favors."

I hope he can hear that same music.

BABY JESUS AND A WAFFLE HOUSE DRUNK

Claremont is eat up with Lutherans.

It's true there's little more than a thousand of us, but we have five churches in 2.5 square miles and two of them are Lutheran. They sit right next to one another on Main Street and favor in brick color and architecture. It's the one question about this town I get asked more than any other.

Why?

I do not know because I don't want to. I just like it that it is, that they go about their Wednesday night spaghetti suppers and Sunday baptisms with only an alley to separate them until comes the holiday season when it's full-on war in the Battle of the Nativities.

St. Marks is elegant, with the appearance of being hand carved and masterfully painted. Mount Calvary believes that size matters. A couple of years ago, in a moment of sacrilege, I stood in the crèche and looked Joseph in the eye.

I'm every bit of 5 feet 10 inches.

St. Marks got sheep but their neighbors have shepherds watching their flock by night. St. Marks has stars and angels and Mt. Calvary has Three Wise Men and two camels. Don't ask me how that third fella got to Bethlehem, but according to the good congregation of Mt. Calvary Lutheran Church, it was not on the humpback of a camel.

For some it may be the end of the Macy's Thanksgiving Day Parade when Santa makes his way down Broadway waving to the crowd, but for me, the sure sign that Christmas is coming is when I see those two Nativities being wrestled into place by Claremont Lutherans. The peace was disturbed one year when the Blessed Redeemer was stolen from the manger at St. Marks. No one noticed until a waitress at the Waffle House in Hickory called the law and said, "There's a drunk standing in the parking lot, holdin' Baby Jesus and cryin'."

I love that story.

The volunteers of the Claremont Appearance Committee drive the streets late in December and decide who deserves the Decoration Awards. I used to be on that committee, but was forced into retirement when I threatened to chain myself to the door unless they presented Avery Hoke with one of the gift certificates for a free pizza. Ask any three-year-old strapped in a car seat and told to "Look, look," as parents drive around town marveling at Christmas décor, and they will tell you, skip the elegance of white lights. Give me an inflatable Snoopy on his dog house and a single strand of big colored bulbs hanging from the gutters. Avery puts a lot of time and effort in a Christmas display I am sure is visible from space. He should get a pizza for it.

Disagreeing with me got a City Council woman quoted in the newspaper when a reporter asked her what she looked for when choosing worthy recipients of free pepperoni. Her answer was that she didn't care to see a lighted plastic Santa in the same yard with a lighted plastic Nativity.

They printed it.

In Claremont, that pretty much insults every other homeowner, and she knew it. She worried and fretted so much that she got in her minivan and drove around town counting how many votes she'd lose in the next election. This gave me and several partners in crime a fine idea.

Well after dark, Kevin Isenhour, me, and the entire Carpenter family (for if you can't involve your children in vandalism, why bother?) drove with our headlights off down a side street and parked. First we stopped the local patrol and told him not to worry if he got a call. He closed his eyes, holding his hand in front of his face. "Don't tell me, Shari. Do whatever you're gonna do but don't tell me."

Kevin works for Duke Power and knew where to plug in the twelve miles of drop cord we'd brought along. Mark and Alisa set Joseph and the Holy Mother in place, and their sweet Katie put the babe in his manger bed. I stood Santa slap in the middle of the new parents and Kevin lit 'em up in the front yard of our elected official.

David Carpenter captured it all on video.

To her credit, our councilwoman with a sense of humor left it up all season and toted it back to me come January. There had been little doubt as to the mastermind of this particular Christmas crime. However, it took a while to sweat a confession out of the Abernathy boys once they made history in the Busbee's yard.

Nobody has better taste than Rita Busbee. She won't admit it but I think she counts the number of lights on the wreath that she hangs on the chimney each year and tops it off with a perfectly tied red velvet bow. White lights twinkle. They don't blink. Everyone knows that blinking is just tacky and twinkling is charming, dammit. Tall spruce trees stand in spotlights, while shorter ones are wrapped in measured strands of white lights, until the whole scene looks like it belongs on one of them commemorative plates my grandmother kept in the china cabinet and wouldn't let me touch. It remained pristine until the Busbees went out of town one December weekend.

The Abernathy boys took the Busbees' tasteful white reindeer and placed them in a compromising position, the doe's animated head bobbing up and down, the buck swaying from side to side. If nothing else, the deer in the Busbee yard were, indeed, having a merry Christmas. It would have been the funniest thing I'd ever seen if Miss Rita didn't one-up them by going to town and buying a baby deer and placing it between the former mated pair. She took pictures, before and after, and mailed them in her Christmas cards.

But sometimes, we're good.

When Russell Boggs told me that he and Mary, his wife of fifty nine years, had always wanted to decorate their Tudor style home in true Williamsburg tradition with live greenery and fruit, candles in every window, but were "too old" to be able to stand on the ladders and brave the cold, we came together as a town and worked for a week in their garage. We wired and pruned until each window was just as Russell had suggested, in his Army chaplain manner, and placed a pineapple at the top of the archway of Leyland cypress greenery over the front door. It looked, for all the world, like the best house in Williamsburg when the local newspaper came to take the picture. Russell and Mary invited everyone for a Christmas Eve open house, where Mary told the story of their courtship in her soft, Southern voice, of roses picked from his mother's garden, of letters written and promises made.

"And I have been in love with him every day of my life since then," she said.

We gathered again a year ago this July past, for Russell, to pray him into the sky and wish for just one more day. Mary wasn't well enough to attend. He left instructions for me to speak, to "quote something from *To Kill A Mockingbird*, and don't forget to be funny." When I think about it, when I can't help it, I remember a moment when the funeral director threw his head back and laughed and another when the mayor sobbed into his hands.

I reckon I did all right.

I helped Christy Sigmon decorate the Hardware and Feed Supply for Christmas today. We tied screwdrivers and packs of batteries on green ribbon and hung them on a tree. We decorated another tree in farm animal ornaments, put it in a washtub, and poured chicken feed around it. We're fairly crafty in Claremont. I drove home past Russell and Mary's house and remembered climbing a ladder to wire up one more set of apples and an orange to satisfy Russell's military need for symmetry, and missed him, missed him bad. I fished through my boxes of decorations and found the handmade paper ornaments Judy Setzer creates and sends in her Christmas cards and smiled a little at what a good sport she was about our midnight raid. She even returned the drop cords. I thought of Avery and the hours of work it takes for him to put out a Christmas display that shames that *Vacation* movie, how he grinned and nodded when the Mayor presented him with an official proclamation of thanks for raising the holiday spirit of Claremont citizens, and I laughed out loud when I remembered asking his Aunt Janie if Avery had told her about it.

"Only forty-nine times," she said.

I pore over magazines and tear out pages for tips and ideas, and work in the cold until my fingers bleed and my house looks like a Christmas card. I appreciate the perfection of Miss Rita's yard, year after year, even if I will never get the sight of fornicating reindeer out of my mind's eye. The thing is, Miss Rita and me, we know that it just doesn't matter. We would not live in a place where every house has white lights and red bows, where music is piped in, and gingerbread houses remain intact from the first of the month through Christmas dinner. Miss Rita and me, we love this place of imperfection, of knockdown-dragout battles over which church has the best damn Nativity, of lawns filled with giant snow globes, and Winnie the Pooh wearing a Santa hat; this place of Baby Jesus and a Waffle House drunk. It is in this place where we buried Russell, where there were so many of us helping the victims of a tornado that the FEMA people were standing around with nothing to do. This is a place where family is defined by choice, and where I am welcome and almost expected at seventeen different tables for Christmas dinner, and every hostess will be wearing a Christmas tree or Santa brooch, the bigger the better. The churches will stagger the times of their Christmas Eve services so you're left with no good excuse for absence. Gaye Morrison will buy me a present but might not get it to me until March. This is the place where I will bake for days and tote it all into The Café for the December birthdays of Larry and Sam. There will be a crowd. A bluegrass band will play "Come Now Angel Band, Come and Around Me Stand."

I know all the words.

YOU ARE HERE

Tana Rasor picked up her beer and came from the front of the room to the back where I was seated at the table furthest from the stage. She barely got a proper hello before she said, "Listen, Terry and I have been talking about you."

A woman with a mission.

She said that there needed to be a new book written on Texas music, that there was an old book but there needed to be a new book and I should think about writing it. She shook her head to emphasize her point when she said, "This ain't Nashville. This is *not* Nashville. You get that, right?"

I really do.

The truck remains in the hands of car mechanics I do not know. If I was home, Danny would be seeing to it that I was taken care of. That's the thing with belonging somewhere. Folks see to you, tend to you. I said to someone, had I been in Claremont, I could have called any one of eight hundred people to come help me when the tire blew and they would have come, all eight hundred. Anyone I didn't call would have known about it before noon the next day, and been mad I hadn't called them. But, I ain't in Claremont.

I'm in Texas.

I have been trying to pay better attention, to understand the differences between this side of that big muddy river and the other, my side. I can see from the map that tells me, "You are Here," the location, but it feels foreign and ill-fitting to me. It's easy to dismiss the places where we don't feel at home as less than the places we do, to lump them in a category of "them" as opposed to "us," and with a wave of the hand, be done. I've never been one to choose easy. It's unlikely I will take that road this time.

I want to understand.

Yankees see the South as one big family. Even if they are too P.C. to call us inbred they think we are alike in how we talk and how we think. That isn't so. There is a difference in a Georgia accent and one from either of the Carolinas, and that Charleston crowd doesn't talk like anyone I have ever shared a table with at the Claremont Café. Though Nashville may be too much of a melting pot to have a way of talking, Tennessee hill people do, and if you think that's not so, listen to my daddy bark at us to get in the kitchen to eat by sayin', "You'uns get in there." As for thinking alike, consider that there are two Lutheran churches sitting side by side on Main Street in Claremont, and they have been there since forever and will be there until The Rapture, both equally sure that one of them will be left behind.

Texas is not the South I know. It is too far west, but that's not it. Not really. A smart and funny friend in North Florida, which ain't really Florida but more Georgia, these being the things you know if you are Southern, said to me that Texas had an identity crisis, that they think they are a country, but they don't have an army so they're confused. They don't seem a bit confused to me. They seem about as sure of themselves as any one group of folks I have ever been around. I think the answer is to be found in the culture.

I've been sitting in the corners of space and maybe a little of time watching people, listening to them, taking notes on what is and is decidedly *not* important to them. It came to me last night when I was editing a piece that Chuck Cannon wrote and sent to me.

Let me say, here and now, that someday folks will line up in a bookstore. They will form a line from the table where he will sit behind a stack of books with a pen in his hand, and they will wait for as long as it takes to get his signature on the inside of the book they clutch to their chest. Chuck is a better writer than I will ever hope to be. Because I love him, I am happy for him. Because I love books, I am happy for everyone who will get to read his river of words that sound in my head more like music than conversation, more like notes than words. Because I wish I was that good, I want to kick him real hard and raise a welt.

I just might do that.

The reason I know he is better is that I understand the language he uses when he writes. It is of my people, our people. In the Southeast we value it, the high pretty in the talk. We have color. We use it. We do not communicate to exchange facts but to sing and to hear that music, to sing that song, a song that is uniquely Southern, that tastes of honey and smells of woodsmoke and peanuts boiling and pork chops frying, and looks like blue sky through pines. We do not use twenty words if we can use two hundred, for that is just sorry.

That is lazy.

God, I love the sound of it. I live for the sound of it, the voice of an old man telling a story, the gestures of women laughing with one another in front of the men, but in the secret world they keep from them; little Southern children asking for a "Yoo Hoo" or a "Coke'cola." It lives on the air, too light to be pulled by gravity, too magical to be confined by the laws of physics or man.

It is of God.

I want to know what god it is that the Texans are of.

I read a collection of short stories some years ago, stories edited by Larry McMurtry. He wrote in his foreword that it took the West longer to develop its writers because their art was channeled differently. His point was that those with creative souls who were born West of the Mississippi used them in ways other than writing, and he had a damn good reason for that. He wrote, "It takes a near perfect descriptive sentence to describe the kinetic joy in watching horses run."

I can understand that. I can't write that sentence. As good as he is, and he's better than me, I don't think Chuck could write that sentence. I have come to believe that McMurtry knew what he was writing about, that Texans had to find other ways to express themselves in a sky this big, a wind this strong. I think they choose to paint, to draw, to try and capture what they saw more than what they felt because words failed them so. There is a wildness, a force of nature; but nature, like everything, is bigger here.

I believe that when their painting failed them too, they turned to music.

I love the music of my people and anyone who says there is a better acoustic guitar player than Reggie Harris *from North Carolina, thank you*, can say so with my boot on their neck. I love the bluegrass. I revere it as well I should, but it stopped. It was satisfied with itself and it stopped. Anyone who tried to advance it was dragged through the mountains by his long hippie hair and called a traitor. Even my own daddy, who still isn't sure that Bill Monroe wasn't at least a distant cousin of our Blessed Redeemer, shakes his head when I demand that he give Sam Bush the credit he deserves. He says, "He can play. No doubt about it. But he don't need all that other stuff. He should just stick to one hundred percent bluegrass and be done with it."

We aren't allowed to say the words "Bela Fleck" without washing our mouths out with soap. Bless his heart.

In Texas, music has a place of honor in the culture. I am trying to decide which came first, the dancing chicken or the swinging egg. Did the land influence the art? Seems like it had to. Did the mountains of my Carolina seem too confining to the people who climbed them, the mighty Mississippi a challenge they had to win to find their place in the dust and the wind and the big sky, the people who decided the Delta blues didn't match their eyes and so chose a different shade, a hue all their own, and named it after the place with more state pride than any Southerners have ever felt. And I should know.

The very word 'Carolina' makes me cry.

I watch Mike Stockton. He helps me to understand this place. Mike is as much made of music as anyone I have met. I have come to believe that he is as much music as my sweet Reggie, and that they are the human illustration of the two sides of The River. In all the places where Reggie is soft, Mike is not. Reggie's hair falls in his eyes. Mike's is like barbed wire. Reggie is round. Mike is tight. Watching him play the bass, I now know what it means to hold up a band, to literally support them and to get no attention or credit for it. I watch his fingers. It's a smooth ride from string to string but if you are not really looking, not really paying attention, Mike disappears on the stage, and that is fine with him. You can just tell. Unless you are duct-taped to a chair in front of the bass player on the stage the next time Mike Stockton plays, you won't remember him, and that would be shameful if he cared what you thought, but he doesn't. That would make him someone else.

That would make him something other than Texan.

I heard a recording of a song he arranged. I have heard that song fifty times. I knew it from first note to last. Mike heard it differently and though I thought I loved it, I know I did not. Mike made it better and he did it in a room by himself, a man and his music, a Texas man and his music.

Tana Rasor, in her reasoning that I should write a book on Texas music, was quick and to the point. She talks like Texas. I am learning that language. She wasn't being short on time or on importance. She only needed to say what she came to say and be done with it. On my side of the river, we sit on porches and talk until we're dead. On this side, they stand on any hill they can find and listen to the wind, brace against it, dare it to knock them down or move them from their chosen ground, but they do it without words. Their defiance is silent, but it is big.

Their language is spoken with strings.

They defined their music with their own chart, their own sound, own name, and stamped "Texas" on all of it. They have used guns and guitars to do their talking. I reckon I can understand that, too. I have to use my words as those are the people I come from, the ones who stayed in the pines. Maybe I can find the words others could not. I think I'd like to try.

The gypsy in me climbed the mountain and crossed the river. Maybe it will help to interpret the language, too.

THE LONELY LITTLE
WALK TO OUR HEARTS

The Shoe Burnin' is a tradition, usually held the Saturday after Thanksgiving unless they feel like changing it, where folks come to tell a story or sing a song about a pair of shoes, only to toss them in the fire afterward. When Grayson Capps wrote a song about the place and included a line about the Shoe Burnin', often explaining it on stage, folks came from as far as New Orleans to witness the soles lost to the flames. It should be on the bucket list of every self-degrading arty type in the South, and it wouldn't surprise me to find it as a secret desire of the more upscale types who make sure to be seen reading *Garden and Gun* in public, preferably in running clothes while drinking a latte before a massage, but after dropping the kids off at private school.

To say that time spent at Waterhole Branch is restorative is like saying that walking on the beach will get sand in your shoes. No matter how tight you lace up, it gets in, the grit and the good.

It finds a way in.

For much of last week, the compound that is Waterhole Branch held my favorite people in the world. If my kids and Matilda and Jack had been there, I'd have locked the gate and thrown the key into the branch where Joe used to swim until the day he found out they weren't lying or drunk when they swore they saw an alligator. The feet that took the lonely little walk to our hearts were shod in flip flops and cowboy boots, tennis shoes and ballet flats, and the Nike sandals Joe cut, then wrapped in duct tape to accommodate the bunion that misshapes his into being Special Needs Feet. The shoes that were burned had walked onto stages to tell stories and sing songs, been spray painted gold for a bride and an "I do," been dragged into the yard by a made-up dog from a made-up one-legged man, and represented the little girl lost to the ugliness of men with holes of nothing where their souls should have been.

It is unnamed and unexplained, the power that lives at Waterhole Branch. I spent time looking at the Spanish moss that hangs in the live oaks. I think it hides there, understanding us, alive with tiny flowers no one notices though there are many, so many. Like us, it blows on the wind and sticks to a limb, hangs on without taking root, growing in sun or shade, sheltering snakes and bats and jumping spiders that scare the devil out of other people when, really, all they're doing is ridding the world of pests that bite at us and leave welts. The moss, like the artists, give the scary things a home, cover in which to disappear, a camouflage of pretty.

Moss has been used as insulation to keep out the cold, stuffing for mattresses that provide rest, and as the insides of voodoo dolls to chase away evil or just poke at it real hard. I think Grayson is made of that moss, but it only shows in his hair. He can keep out the cold. Everyone feels a little warmer when he sings. The story written and read by Jennifer Horne gave her character a soft place to live, a humor that let her cope with life's disappointments in men and in Republicans. Chuck Cannon's songs poke holes in the evil that scares us, stick enough pins in it that it changes shape and looks less like a burden we alone are bearing and more like one we can share.

Joan Harrell might be made more of the live oak limb that catches the moss, steady and strong and there to support, growing as she needs to, first in this direction, then in that, to adapt to the changes in light. Joe is that space between, both bark and moss, an endless distance to navigate, an impossible journey to deny. Lari White is the shiny moss, the iridescent strings that catch the light and reflect it back. Michael is the tangle, the places where singer/songwriter/storyteller/writer/performer form a net to hold it all. Susan Cushman is the fragile but constant connection to the host, knowing she belongs, refusing to let go, working, working to get a better hold. Chuck Jones is the breeze that goes in and out of the places that seem too small for anything of importance to fit through. He finds a way, wafting through and carrying the tiny seeds to the next branch where they can go and become another rootless web of flowers and snakes. He even knew the baby's name was Micah. Chris Clifton and Suzanne Hudson are the flowers, hiding, surprising when truly seen, afraid no one will notice, uncomfortable and exposed when they do.

And I am the watcher, the one who sits beneath the branches to look and to listen, to understand them, to find their role and help them if they forget how to hold on to the tree or to one another.

Grayson wrote it, the line in the song, "It's a lonely little walk to our hearts, lonely like the morning stars." All that is harder outside its confines is made easier at Waterhole Branch, a little bit easier. Maybe it is less lonely a walk because we have each other. Maybe it is softened up by the sandy lane. Maybe it's the Spanish moss, the chain of inconspicuous flowers and rootless life, the strength to hold on, the freedom to fly, the insulation against the bitter, the safest of exposures.

I don't know.

I know this. Grayson sings…

"My love for you is comin' down. And, my love for you is comin' down."

SACRED GROUND

Michael Reno Harrell told me this story about a bandmate of his, a long while ago. He said he wanted to paint the Texas flag on the side of a barn. Texans are like that. Most of the South is closed off to thinking that anything that happens outside the lines drawn by them two Mason-Dixon boys has any real significance to our lives. I had a good looking boy from Missouri with long, curly hair once tell me that he didn't consider North Carolina a part of "the real South," and that was the last time I considered him at all.

A sense of place is easy to come by and impossible to hang onto when your soul is made of gypsy winds and angel wings. The songs that play in your head aren't of "on the solid rock I stand," but only of highways and leaving. Anything that holds too tight is a trap. Besides, you carry the holy stuff in your own head, in a heart made of dog-eared road maps and a carpetbag that no matter how heavy can always hold more, no matter how worn and threadbare, keeps packing it in.

I have walked in the Holy Land. I have stood on sacred ground. Its solid rock is a wall and the author of its Good Book said all she needed to the first time, and never needed to repeat herself.

It pisses me off that it's set in Monroeville, Alabama, but that's where it is.

A year before the flames took the only home I ever felt was mine, I loaded the truck and headed for Mobile Bay and a gathering of poets and drunks, one and the same in almost every instance. I added two hours to the trip by skipping Atlanta and going through the mountains, my mountains, more to be in that place where Carolina meets Tennessee than to avoid sixteen lanes of asphalt in a town that no more belongs to the South than unsweet tea. It comes and goes quick-like, that place, that state line, that river where eagles fish to feed their babies nesting in pines that grow up through clay and rock because they can.

It's worth the extra time.

Turning left in Knoxville, through Chattanooga, and Birmingham, and Montgomery, where Sister Rosa said "enough is enough" and held to it, I came up on the Hank Williams Lost Memorial Highway. Sonny Brewer, a writer and editor I used to know pretty good, called and asked where I was and how much longer I would be. He had the keys I needed to The Writer's Cottage that he swears is haunted, and two teenage boys to tote to school functions, and music lessons on a list of things not to mess up from his wife who usually tended to such things. He figured on the general time I would arrive and said he'd meet me at that famous bookstore where Miss Betty Joe lives upstairs.

That was before I saw the sign.

If I took the exit, I would be late. If I passed it up, I'd arrive on time and wouldn't contribute to any excuse Sonny might come up with for not doing things the right way Diana always does. I checked the rear-view mirror and hit the turn signal. The sign said it would be less than twenty miles before I got there. If you can't go an extra seventeen miles you deserve to live without salvation and can't nobody help you after that.

I sat on the steps of the Monroeville Courthouse and thought of Atticus and what he had taught me at a time when there wasn't much of anybody still trying to tell me anything. I called Margaret Garrison but she wasn't home. I left a message that I was there, on those steps. I might have been crying, but I don't think so. Everything in town was closed, which made it better. I had Atticus and Tom Robinson and the children hiding in the bushes across the street all to myself.

I thought of Mrs. Ross handing me the book that made me a writer, though I didn't know that at the time. I remembered her demanding that we understand why Jem's name was what it was. I remembered her insisting that we come to know that Tom and Boo are not the only mockingbirds to be found between the covers of that book. I remembered that I didn't return it when we were asked to leave them on the corner of her desk. I stole it good, and for the first time I realized she might have known that and let me walk out the door with it tucked in my purse, the one with the peace sign sticker on the flap. Mrs. Ross might have known that I needed it more than the county school system.

When I was ready, I climbed back in the truck and drove around the corner to the one-way street that leads out of town. Someone later asked me if I tried to find *her*. I did not. To thank her is to not try to thank her. She wanted it that way and if that is what she wants, she earned the right to it. As I drove, I saw a rock wall, once a part of a garden, but now just an empty lot of grass and nothing else. I remembered the description in the book, the wall made of rocks and mortar where children played and acted out scenes from the books they read, *Tom Swift* and *Grey Ghost*. I knew that the odds of that rock wall being their rock wall were slim to none but I pulled over, anyway. I parked in the lot of a summer-only ice cream shop, closed for the season, and I sat on the wall.

I thought of that little boy, smaller than the others, dressed funny and fussed over by half crazy aunts and ignored by his own momma. I know how he felt. I thought of the little girl in overalls who wanted to be like the boys, of how clearly she saw mockingbirds, especially ones with broken wings and hearts, when others only found them noisy and bothersome. I wondered if she felt that insight to be a blessing or a curse.

Most times I couldn't say, but I sure do know how that feels, too.

I know I cried sitting on that wall. I thought of the stories of blankets wrapped around cold children standing in front of a burning house, of Halloween nights, of grass harps, and Christmas Eves, all the words perfectly strung together and placed on the page, written by the children who played in the heat of Alabama summers when they grew to be two-thirds of the Holy Trinity, with Faulkner, sure, of what is Southern writing, good writing, the best writing. I thought of what that has meant to the lives of all of us looking, searching for something to believe in when hellfire and damnation just don't make all that much good sense.

I whispered, "Thank you" softly enough so that she couldn't hear it, but might could feel it somehow.

It was then that I saw the sign. It had the shape of a historical marker they put along the road to tell us that Yankees beat the fire out of some Confederate boys on the very spot where the sign went in the ground, in case we were to forget we still have some whuppin' up on to do.

I don't know why I didn't see it, driving by. I wasn't looking, I suppose. I only saw the wall. When I stood in front of the sign and read that this was it, the childhood home of Truman Capote, that the house had burned away some years before, I knew that I was there, on Sacred Ground, and the rock wall now stained with the melted cones and fudgesicles of children too young to eat fast the way their momma said to, had once been their stage, Nelle's and Truman's. It had once been a mighty ship or a dark cave or any world they could pull from the pages of the books they read before they wrote their own and gave them to us.

On that solid rock, I stand.

Before I got to Fairhope, I considered which lie to tell, that I got tired or that I had car trouble. I thought of what would get me hollered at by Sonny the least, and decided it was being too sleepy and needing to pull over for a bit before I could trust myself to drive the rest of the way. The risk to life and the certainty of my own death seemed a better excuse for being late than a flat tire.

When I got out of the truck, Sonny was stomping mad and yelling, "God damn ye. What took so long?"

I said, "I went to Monroeville."

Sonny's face lost its scarlet color and his eyes went soft.

"Well, I don't blame ye. Here are the keys. Don't mind the ghosts."

I never do.

FOOD

My maternal grandmother burned every piece of meat she ever fried. Bless her heart. It went from mooing to shoe leather right there in her skillet. Despite preparing three meals a day for my grandfather and whatever farm hand or family was there, and they were always there, she really wasn't a very good cook. Now, her homemade noodles were legendary. All others pale in comparison but those were reserved for holiday dinners, when instead of the fried potatoes she fixed at least twice a day every day, the potatoes were mashed so we could pile them noodles over the top and know it was Christmas.

I love mashed potatoes.

If I was denied wedding cake and chocolate chip cookies and home-made peach ice cream and Snickers bars from now until they throw my ashes off a Carolina mountaintop, I would be just fine, grouchy, maybe, but fine. Take away my mashed potatoes and you will know the Biblical definition of wrath. I need them. For the eight months and eight days I carried Walker, mashed potatoes was the only food that stayed down long enough to keep me from starving.

Walker loves mashed potatoes, too.

I was taught to measure so I could enter the baking competition at the county fair. It was a requirement for respectable girls from the farm land to pick out the six best matching cookies, place them on paper doilies so they would look fancy on Dixie brand paper plates, wrestle a sheet of Saran Wrap over them, and wait to be named the Grand Champion so you could do it all over again for the State Fair. I got a blue ribbon, but the girl down the road got to tote her secret recipe to the Big City when all she'd done was add the nuts listed as "optional" on the bag of chocolate chips. One of my aunts said she was sure she used the milk chocolate chips instead of what every good baker in the county knew was right, which was the semi-sweet. That girl always was a little uppity. I got my picture made and printed on Page 3 of the local newspaper holding the canned beets that took the Grand Champion prize in Food Preservation, and didn't have to do another damn thing to get them ready for the State Fair seeing as how they were preserved and all.

I was taught to measure but I learned to cook on my own. I wanted more. I read cookbooks like they were novels, especially on Sunday mornings during Meet the Press. I learned to fix all the things my people couldn't have imagined eating. I grilled salmon and seared tuna and shopped at the famed Atlas Grocery for the hard to find ingredients, where on one shopping trip Abbie and I listened to two old ladies on their way to Temple determined not to pay the eight dollars they found too high for a true New York style cheesecake. One said, "Get the Philly, Margie. We'll make it ourselves."

I bought a cookbook with pictures, *Great Friends, Good Dinners*, that gave me entire meals to cook from appetizer to dessert. Abbie and I called it "Shitty Friends, Fabulous Dinners" or "Decent Enough Friends, Crazy Good Dinners." I found a second copy, used, and ordered it for her when she married. Abbie does beautiful prep work. She takes more care with that than I. But I got to be such a good cook, so thorough at understanding food, I no longer needed the tutorial of having the meal planned. I could dream up my own menu and serve it up to my friends, shitty or decent enough.

Ham and mashed potatoes with gravy, green bean and mushroom soup casserole with the crunchy onions on top, and macaroni and cheese were and are still among my favorites, food I still needed, depended upon for comfort and memories more than sustenance, but it wasn't enough. I needed new and different flavors. When I traveled, I watched friends drive themselves to the brink of tears trying to find American food in a foreign land. Not me, I wanted the goulash in the Czech Republic, the sausage in Germany, and the longing for more of the lobster bisque in Lucerne, Switzerland still haunts me.

My stepmother is a great cook. Whatever it is that she does to a turkey draws Walker to the table like a crack junkie to the pipe. He can't stop even if it kills him. A few Thanksgivings ago, he lay in the floor, miserable and moaning. Before he went to bed he was back, his head stuck in the fridge, peeling away the foil and picking meat off the bones with his fingers. He loves turkey. He loves my turkey, but when you asked him why he likes Myrna's so much better, he says, "It's different."

That's fine by me. I understand.

I took a dessert to a family dinner a long, long time ago when there remained enough family to bother with a holiday meal, and before I realized just how unwelcome I had become. I baked a flourless chocolate cake, the recipe right out of that fancy cookbook I had learned so much from. I drizzled chocolate syrup over the cake and let it run in pretty twists and turns on the cake plate beneath it. I shaved solid chocolate just like I saw them do on the Food Network and placed the curls just so on the top. I stuck one perfect strawberry, perfectly dipped in chocolate in the middle of the curls, balanced it in a cardboard box, and strapped it into the truck with the seat belt to insure a safe arrival.

An aunt who isn't really an aunt said it was wonderful, fawning over my presentation and the flavor. The comments from others I most remember had to do with me not being satisfied with the traditional chocolate sheet cake that has held a place on our family dinner table since the beginning of time, good enough for everyone else in the family since it was first placed in the dessert section of the Formica countertop at the end of the line right before the sweet tea and ice-filled Tupperware glasses. When a cousin once added a teaspoon of cinnamon in the batter, it was seen as coming from The Devil's own hand, and she stopped that shit right quick like.

I love that cake. I bake that cake. I wanted more. I have learned that it hurts folks, folks I never mean to hurt, and still, I don't know how to stop wanting it, that thing called *more*.

I kept getting emails about my fun in the sun, how lucky I am to be in Key West. What I most look forward to is sitting on hard wooden barstools I have to turn sideways to best fit my ass, in a not so sunny corner so I can talk and listen to John and Sally. I enjoy the people with the shot glasses in their hand. I laugh at their jokes because they're funny, but by seven o'clock, I'm looking forward to the arrival of John, who usually gets to The Smokin' Tuna first, and Sally.

Charlie Bauer took me to breakfast to meet a man named Dink who lived in Key West in the time of McGuane and Harrison and Brautigan and, my favorite-favorite, Guy de la Valdene, so I could write a better magazine story. I talked with Elizabeth about the importance of community in child rearing, and with Eddie about Louisville basketball, and sitting in a waiting room while a doctor sticks wires in the heart of someone you're not sure you can live without. Donna Bruton made me laugh so hard I nearly peed in my pants, right there in one of them sideways wooden barstools, and she showed me pictures of her granddaughters and talked of how different they are than one another, and how different a grandmother she is. Her love is not less. Her wishes for their happiness are not fewer than those of a constant, doting grandmother—not less, just different.

Then I met Ericson.

We spent an evening listening to Chris play with Carl Wagoner, a guitar player who claims Chris is his idol. While they played, we listened. When they stopped, we talked. We talked about Carl playing on the same stage with Chris, and the days when he would stare at him, at the movement of the pick, the bend of the strings. He still does, but he watches now to match him, to play *with* him. We talked about a community of artists, of musicians and songwriters and literary types, and how important it is to find one another and stick together. I told him of Waterhole Branch, of Joe and Suzanne, of the Shoe Burnin' project, of the way we are when we are all in the same place, and how much better our art becomes because of having been there.

Ericson said, "It's like food. We need to be fed and to feed each other. It's how we keep going, keep making better art, better music."

It is exactly that.

I'm often accused of not being satisfied. It's not that things aren't good enough; it's that I need to have other parts of me fed. That makes some people feel that they are not good enough, they are less than others. That isn't so. I know better. I love the people I write about and if that isn't clear to them, I am doing a bad job. I envy the people who can stay in one place, can be happy with things the way they are, while I am looking at the door, eyeing the street, wondering what the food tastes like at a café somewhere else.

I remember sitting with Michael Reno Harrell in the Claremont Café, him telling me, "Nobody wants to talk about writing. I don't get to talk about this. I drive down the mountain to sit in this Café and talk to you about writing because I need it." He came to The Café for me, a little bit for the cheeseburgers, but he came down the mountain for me to feed him a bigger helping of a dish called "why we write." I came to The Café for the people I could write about. They are more than good enough for me. They are better people than I will ever be at near about everything. Mostly, they are better at being. I am bad at being. I look for a different way to be, a different where to be. I look for more food while loving every bite of the meal I am being served. I recognize that it is hard to keep me fed, and I am not saying that is the reason that the barstools at The Smokin' Tuna didn't fit me. They did fit me. Only, I had to turn them a different way.

Someone who will never understand and therefore never like me very much said something about a friend of mine, a friend I love just about as much as I love anyone who ain't Chris and ain't my kids. He was talking about my friend and said, "He needs the stage. He requires constant attention."

I shot back so fast I did not know the next word that was coming out of my mouth before I, my own self, heard them. "No, he doesn't. He requires interaction, not attention." And then I said things about why my friend was more than likely bored that are too ugly to repeat, things I shouldn't oughta said, but I tend to be wired that way when defending my people.

What I should have said is what Ericson said. What I should have said is, he needs to be fed. He needs to keep up a steady diet of creativity and wonder and to test himself, to see if he can write it pretty just one more time, if he can write it prettier than the last time he wrote it pretty. It's how he, no—it's how we feel alive and worthy of taking in oxygen.

It's why we get up in the morning. We love mashed potatoes and chocolate sheet cake. We write love songs and stories about peeling the potatoes and melting the chocolate and the sound of the mixer and the look on Papaw's face when he would take a bite, having waited since last Christmas for noodles.

But if we seem anxious to leave, it isn't that we believe there is better food at somebody else's table. We're trying to find each other. We're trying to feed something else. The world looks different to us. We tend to want to see more of it. Love us anyway. Keep the mashed potatoes warm and the sheet cakes covered up until we get back.

That is what I should have said.

Nancy Mayhew came across the bar and grabbed my arm, pointed to a group of four women, high school friends of hers who came to Key West for a visit. Every one of them spoke Carolina. I know that sound, that delicious sound of phrasing and cadence, funny Carolina women out for an adventure at the end of the world. They were all going home the next day.

But they weren't eating mashed potatoes and for dessert, they had ordered Key Lime pie.

And you know what?

We were invited to have Easter dinner with Carl's family. His beautiful and funny wife, Erin, and I competed, who had the best redneck holiday stories to tell, and while she shared a hilarious story about her trip to Graceland, or Mecca, as my people see it, I knew from Sally that Erin had been to the Dr. Martin Luther King museum while she was in Memphis, that she had insisted they go to the hotel and see where he dreamed his last dream. Ericson came to dinner, too. It was a patchwork family, put together on Easter Sunday, a few hours before most of them would take a stage and play music for people who came to hear them, and many, many more who tuned in on their computer screens to listen to artists who need each other and go in search of the food they need to play or to write or to paint or to sculpt...artists who, just hours before, had eaten ham, macaroni and cheese, green beans and mushroom soup casserole with the crunchy onions on top, and mashed potatoes, and for dessert, there wasn't a chocolate sheet cake to be found. We had pretty little Easter cupcakes.

I saved the plastic carrot from the top of mine to put in my wooden box of memories.

THE WAY YOU BURN ME, BABY, I SHOULD BE ASHES BY NOW

My left arm is in a soft cast. There's a fairly significant gash on my right arm and what my mamaw called a "goose egg" on my forehead. One knee looks like somebody swung a tire iron and hit me square. The other isn't so bad, really, other than tiny bruises and the scars from a bicycle accident when I was eight and the cinders left lodged under the skin from not using peroxide like I was told to do.

These injuries are a direct result of the renovations happening at Waterhole Branch in Fairhope, Alabama. Stuff falls, or I fall, or run into the stuff that fell. I'm a good painter. I am a lousy climber. I'm great at designing a room, laying it out so pretty it could be the featured story in *Country Living* magazine. I am profoundly bad at waiting for someone to help me move the furniture.

I'm bad at waiting.

Chris will walk into a room and stare at me like I'm a disobedient child. This stare is followed by, "You don't *listen*. You will (pause) not (pause) *listen*," then a speech about how he will help me if I will just come and get him and tell him what I need. That speech, in all its many forms, usually lasts while he is helping guide a couch or a table or a piano in place and sometimes it lingers into the moment that should be my glory, the euphoria of standing back and beholding my brilliant design. He is rarely amused when the first thing I say in response to his big finish, "And then you get hurt and that wouldn't happen if you would let me help you," is, "Look at that (couch/table/piano). I am a genius."

I really am.

We're preparing for a video shoot, a sort of mini-documentary to better explain *The Shoe Burnin'*. I'm working on the home of Joe Formichella and Suzanne Hudson, well-known and gifted Southern writers. Among the many fine qualities that Joe and Suzanne possess is the admirable fact that they can walk the earth free of guilt as to its demise, innocent of having caused any damage to the environment because they, the both of them, the two of them, neither of them have ever contributed one blessed thing to the landfill. They have kept every scrap of paper on which they have written a grocery list, a doctor's appointment, an idea for a book, a story, a title, a lead, an ending, and if not for my swift and razor sharp intervention you would have seen them on an upcoming episode of *Hoarders*, or read of them some years from now while standing in line at the grocery store, on the front page of *The Star* in a headline like: "Southern Literary Greats Found Buried in Their Own Words."

They're good people. They are. You might remember they married on Fat Tuesday after eight years of living in sin—and among what has to be a record number of spiral notebooks and reams of printer paper—so that the day would be of a happy memory, and not a reminder of the day Suzanne lost her brother, Wilson, to the cancer they are sure came from his work in cleaning the Gulf, a spill that the rest of the world forgets about when they pull up to a green and white gas pump to fill their tank. It is like them, finding a way to cope with loss by creating something new, in this case, a wedding to be remembered.

Joe promised to let Suzanne die first so she wouldn't have to tend to him if he was all bedridden and feeble, and Suzanne promised Joe she would never ask him to do yard work. Then they were pronounced man and wife by Miss Nelle's beloved preacher, Tom Butts. Grayson Capps, in a wife beater and jeans with holes in the knees, sang the wedding march and his daddy, wearing a tux, gave a toast about what a bad idea marriage was. That took care of the Capps family's duties. Joe and Suzanne will celebrate their anniversary on Fat Tuesday no matter what the date is, so they don't have to remember what the date is; a foolproof plan.

Chris and I are staying in their guest cottage while I paint and design and redesign and turn their home into a showplace. It's a trial run of sorts to see if it fits us, the cottage and the community. Chris practices his music most of the day except for the time it takes to give the speech about me not listening and tending to my wounds, and plays on the stages from the Florida line to the other side of Mobile Bay at night. It's a pretty happy life made happier yesterday, because I actually asked him for help.

You would have thought I handed him a Grammy.

I asked him to help me move a china cabinet away from the wall so I could paint behind it. Suzanne had set a bunch of stuff on the floor in front of it, things she took off the shelves I was painting the day before, books, decorative bowls, jars, an old telephone, and a soldier's helmet, either German or Russian, I don't remember which. Chris was picking the things up off the floor and setting them on a side table, making a point of his willingness to help, and how that due to his assistance I would not be maimed by falling oak cabinets, or impaling myself on the spike in the helmet. This was his moment, a life lesson, a teaching tool, and all I had to do to know he had been right all along was to look at his happy face as he picked up the books, the picture frames, the Mason jar, and the candy dish, and placed them on the table. See? See how helpful, how much faster, how much easier the entire process goes when help is requested and allowed and freely given?

"What's in this jar?" he asked.

"I don't know. Probably sand from some beach trip. They save every damn thing."

"It's in the candy dish, too."

"Another stupid trip to the beach, I reckon."

Chris wouldn't let me move the cabinet until we moved the antique clock, the one Joe wants to remain broken so it won't chime. As Chris looked for a safe place to put the Regulator, Suzanne emerged from the bedroom where I had banished her until she went through the boxes and drawers and threw away the sandals with the broken strap she wore her junior year in college. She rushed to make room on the table for the clock and rearranged the items Chris had just placed there from the floor. As she picked up the candy dish, Chris, his arms full of a hundred-year-old clock, asked, "What is in there, Suzanne?"

"Wilson."

"Your brother? In the candy dish?"

"Yeah, the Mason jar, too, but that better suits him."

On Saturday, some of Wilson's friends are coming over to finish the wall of whiskey bottles cemented in his honor. Suzanne will empty the candy dish but not the Mason jar. She promised to take some of him back to Georgia where they were born. As she held up the ashes of Wilson Hudson, her brother who chose to go fishing and ride on a Mardi Gras float instead of taking the chemo, which would result in the same ending, though slower and uglier, Suzanne said, "He was just a little bitty thing. We've already thrown some of him out around the Whiskey Wall, but this is what's left."

And people ask me if I ever want to write fiction.

POUND CAKE
AND MISS PEGGY

Wherever she was going, something somewhere required her immediate attention.

She didn't stroll or pump her arms like the women who wear yoga pants and Sketchers and carry lavender weights in their perfectly manicured hands, their ponytails swinging from side to side. She passed my house nearly every day, often early, and I would tell myself that if she were wearing pink, it would be a good day.

She always wore pink.

It seemed to be her signature color. Her hair was snow white and kept short, for she was a busy woman, you could just tell, and hairdos and hours at the beauty shop would have been wasted time.

I would most often see her through the windows in my front room, what must have once been the parlor. It had a bay window, uncharacteristically fancy for the town and the time it was built, around the turn of the century. An ornate mantel with carved spindles and a beveled mirror surrounded the coal-burning fireplace, and the floors made of wide plank pine, stained rich, had darkened with age. The ceiling had been lowered and covered in some sort of man-made carcinogenic tile, and drywall had been nailed and spackled over the beadboard walls. The exception was the original wainscoting, now painted a dingy cream. The previous owners of the house, a couple from Minnesota, whose accent had made it impossible to get through the closing without imagining that I had stepped into a Cohen brothers film, had painted every room either hunter green or burgundy, both colors in the kitchen, but the parlor was the latter, making it dark and cave-like. I didn't brighten that atmosphere when I hung heavy curtains at those bay windows so as not to be seen from either of the two streets that bordered my corner lot.

I chose the house before I stepped inside. It was love at first sight. I told the realtor that if it had any sort of a decent kitchen, I wanted it. She told me that no one had made an offer because it only had two bedrooms, and trains ran all night, every night, along the tracks at the back of the property and that I should think about it before I laid claim to it. She smelled of too much perfume in a failed attempt to cover her habit of smoking like a chimney, a trick my grandmother had taught me to recognize from the third row of Normanda Christian Church. I signed the offer despite the obvious failings of my new home and its lack of an enthusiastic saleswoman.

Walker met the lady in pink long before I did. He started school at Claremont Elementary and had begged me to let him walk the two blocks "like the other kids." He was escorted to Main Street one day by Miss Peggy. He knew her name because he asked. He told me of their conversation. "I told that lady down the street, the one with the dachshund dog, that she had pretty flowers and Miss Peggy said I was a kind child."

Miss Peggy, who could recognize a boy with nothing to hide when she saw one, had questioned my son. "She asked me if you had a husband. I said, no. You don't have a husband, do you, Momma?"

I did not have a husband.

I had had one by my nineteenth birthday, a distant man, a good man who went from long-haired hippie boy with a brief stint in Monterey to hearing his name called to serve the Lord. I did not hear such a call and so we had sat together on the floor of our living room and divided up the household goods. He wanted me to take the stereo and the albums because I loved music so much and I said if that were the case, he should get the biggest of the two televisions. No one told us we were supposed to hate each other, so we didn't. We had a baby daughter to think about and despite him being washed deep in the blood of the Lamb and me swimming hard to free myself of it, we had gotten on pretty good all those years. The summer before Abbie turned five, he married a woman I liked and respected. She lost a baby, only months before I had Walker. I handed my week old son to her when they came to pick up Abbie, then nearly twelve, for a weekend visit. She sat in a rocking chair and cried, and I cried with her. Jody was good to my child, often more of a mother to her than I was, and when Abbie married, we decorated the church together and cooked many Thanksgiving dinners in our daughter's tiny kitchen.

I went through a number of disasters that included, but was not limited to, a teacher who liked his students a little too much, and the heir to a hardware business who made fun of the way I said "insurance" with the accent on the first syllable because, I suppose, he enjoyed reminding folks that he was slumming. There was a narcissistic doctor whom I married for all the wrong reasons, though two of those reasons were blonde and called Abbie their sister and when I looked at them then, and think of them now, it's basketball and soccer games and birdhouses painted in Dalmatian spots, and Looney Tunes and Warren Zevon songs wailed from the back seat, and love in grass stained T-shirts that I hold onto— and the knowledge that Walker was born, and despite our unintentional efforts to take it from him, remained the best that was in all of us. He got only the good and for that, there can be no regrets.

I followed up a narcissist with a sociopath and called it quits. I came to Claremont to get my boy grown and be alone. Forever.

"No, Walker, I don't have a husband."

"Miss Peggy does."

He was right. Miss Peggy sure did.

In 1946, Peggy Little had walked to the soda shop in Claremont, North Carolina with her best friend, Norma Jean Phifer. Jim Campbell, a boy she'd been baptized with, said for her to wait on him to get his hair cut and he'd walk her home. The sailor sitting in the corner whose daddy had signed him up for the Navy, just home from The War, spoke up.

"No. I'm gonna walk her home."

Steve Miller wanted a date for Jim Carpenter's party the next Saturday night. Peggy told him she was already going, so she reckoned she could go with him, and he reckoned that was right. He got a job as a brakeman on "the local" that ran on the tracks from Asheville to Spencer and in the courtship that followed, Peggy, sitting on the back steps, polishing her shoes, heard the train whistle and ran so fast, taking a short cut down Clove Sigmon's driveway, past the ditch at the mill where they dyed the socks, that she fell in.

He bought her a diamond anyway.

Steve was known to all the fellers in town as Hambone. In service to his country, Hambone had learned a thing or two he wasn't quite ready to forget and on one of those train routes to Asheville, he answered when temptation called his name. Peggy found out about it, breaking the engagement and Hambone's heart. Without his Peggy, it seemed the only thing to do was go back to the Navy, so Steve Miller left Claremont and took to writing to Peggy.

She ignored his letters of apology. She went to the Junior-Senior prom with Jim Carpenter. She graduated high school and got a job at The White Pine. This is what she told me:

"I didn't apply for the job. I would have liked to go to college but my mother was without any help, working in the hosiery mill to keep us up. We lived with my grandmother, and it was no more than right for me to give up on college to stay at home and tend to her. Well, Noah McGee owned The White Pine, and he asked my mother if I could come work for him and if she would allow it, he would come pick me up, every shift, and see to it that I got home."

Miss Peggy told me it was a swanky place with a band that played on Wednesday and Saturday nights. She was too smart to switch nights with anyone, working on Wednesdays when the crowd from The Silver Moon came in. She knew they were better tippers. She was dating Jim Sigmon, who also worked at The White Pine. They were making salads when he asked her, "Have you seen him?"

It had been two years, two years of disciplinary notices and unanswered letters, but Hambone was back.

When Peggy walked into the dining room, he was there, waiting to talk to her she was too busy. He asked what time she got off work. She told him that didn't matter because Noah McGee drove her home after work.

Steve Miller said, "Ain't no damn McGee takes you home tonight."

Peggy answered, "Fine. But I'm not talking to you with them curly-cues on that moustache."

When he came back for her at the end of the night, his handlebar moustache was gone. Forest Pope had snipped off the ends at the Pool Room.

He had lost the wedding band he bought for her the first time she said yes and had to buy another. Her momma cried and said she oughta know he was not done sowing his wild oats, but Peggy rightly believed he was. Mrs. Murray at the Claremont Florist decorated the church and made the bouquets. Peggy wore a dress and veil she borrowed from Steve's sister, Honey, and all of Honey's bridesmaids loaned their dresses to Peggy's attendants, all except her maid of honor, Norma Jean, who wore the dress Peggy would wear the next Sunday when she sang at *her* wedding. Steve didn't have a dress uniform. That had to be borrowed, too. Peggy carried a white Bible and an orchid.

They honeymooned at the Robert E. Lee Hotel in Winston-Salem after which Steve went back to the ship. He came home, for good, in 1950, with the tattoo of a nekkid woman on his arm covered with the tattoo of a snake, for Peggy's sake. His grandmother, a good Christian woman, would have disapproved of any sort of tattoo, so he wore nothing but long sleeves in her presence, even in the Augusts of Carolina summers, until she died in 1985, "never knowing he had a mark on his body."

Miss Peggy laughed when she told me that.

Steve drove to Flint, Michigan, and bought an Alma mobile home, brand new, and pulled it to Claremont. "Oh, we thought we had a mansion," Peggy said. They parked it in Richmond, Virginia, when he worked for Dupont, and in Barnwell, South Carolina, when he worked at the hydrogen bomb plant, and in Claremont when they came home and Steve took a job driving trucks for the man who'd shaved off his handlebars, Forest Pope. Peggy stayed home and mothered Doug and Jane, forging Steve's name on his paycheck every week when she took it to the bank, and did as he asked of her in calling his attention to his vocabulary.

He was the best cusser in town.

Jo Marilyn Hewitt has told me many times of Hambone's cussin'. She said he was so good at it that nobody much noticed. It was just the way he talked, how he expressed himself. Miss Peggy said she never cared, one way or the other, though it seemed to irritate him. "He just couldn't be bothered to stop."

When Steve retired, they bought a fifteen-foot Scotty camper and headed south to Highway 10 in Florida, driving straight across the country to California. They even went to Hollywood. Before they were through they saw every state but Alaska and Hawaii, and came on home to Claremont to build a little two bedroom house on Yount Street. Steve picked up trash on his daily walks and was recognized by the mayor for doing so. Peggy was named "Mother of the Year" and "Citizen of the Year" and was a founding member of the Friends of the Claremont Library before anybody thought there might, someday, be a library in such a little town.

Steve repaired small engines, lawnmowers and the like. He began to forget how to put them back together, but Peggy didn't worry about that.

"I just thought he'd gotten quieter."

It took the insistent love of lifelong friends, Leiter and Lottie Pannel, to make Peggy promise to take him to Dr. Ross's office and be told what they already knew. He took medicine that made his stomach hurt so badly he would roll on the floor in pain, but it didn't help him remember the names of his children or how to drive a route he had taken three times a week for years and years. He asked Peggy, "Who was that nice lady?" when his daughter kissed him goodbye and said, "Babe, that Doug knows every road in the county," never remembering that it was he, his daddy, who taught him the way.

Still, he never forgot his Peggy. He could call her name and wanted her hand in his until his last breath.

Miss Peggy walked three miles a day and volunteered for every committee, club, and project in our end of Catawba County. She made her famous pound cakes to feed the volunteers at the blood drive, the heart drive, the cancer drive, for spina bifida research, for the Lutheran Altar Guild, the quilting mission, the church breakfasts, the church suppers, and every reason for a bake sale the school could dream up.

And when she opened up her water bill and saw the notice inviting anyone wanting to help bring a library to Claremont to come to the meeting, she baked a lemon pound cake and went to city hall.

I didn't.

It would take me three years, three years of watching the lady in pink walk by my house, the house I used as armor, three years of seeing her,

a woman who recognized the kindness in my child because he compli-
mented the gardening skills of a neighbor I never spoke to. It would take
three years and pneumonia and a book and a phone call before I would
walk into a meeting of the Friends of the Claremont Library and meet
Miss Peggy Miller.

She baked a pound cake on account of she heard I was coming.

She told me this love story one warm day on her front porch while
she crocheted hats for poor children. The ladies of Mt. Calvary Lutheran
Church had set a goal as a group, of making one hundred hats before
winter. Miss Peggy was on her forty-fifth. Pink geraniums were planted
in a pot on the table between us.

She said she did not know why I kept my hair so long and couldn't
imagine the time it took out of each day "just to mess with all that hair."

She had baked a pound cake for Naomi White's eighty-fifth birthday and sent it with her sister, Clara, who told Miss Peggy that she said,
"Thank you, Jesus" when they gave it to her. Thinking of that made Miss
Peggy smile. She had another one cooling on the kitchen counter to give
to Harley and Libby Brown in exchange for the apples they were bringing
to her. She wasn't about to accept them empty-handed.

Miss Peggy told me that she had been thinking about Steve's father,
how in his later years he once told them that he couldn't believe how
so much of his time was spent going to funerals. "Now," she said, "I go.
Now it's me who goes to so many, many funerals."

EVERY DAY SINCE

I don't know when I have had better news.

It came from Andrea Busbee. She gave it to me straight, as she is a no-nonsense kind of girl, and she knew I needed to hear it and she knew exactly how I would take it.

Mary Boggs has died.

The disease that took from her the scrapbook kept in memory, that tore from her the pages of the life she led, the lives she touched, the good done at her hand, the world she helped to change was not powerful enough to take from her manners. Her pleases and thank yous were still there. She still offered you tea even though she had no way to serve it to you. Her apologies for her failing memory still showed the grace that was her mark on the world, on the places she lived, on my little town.

She was still Mary.

She was, without question, the kindest, most genuinely good person I have ever known and ever will. She was blind to the bad in any of us, in all of us. If she had to choose that, to not see our failings, she did so in a way that seemed effortless, a way that made, even you, believe they

247

were not there, that you were only made of the goodness and light that I am sure was more reflecting off Mary than could ever really live in me, for I know that I did not deserve Mary's belief in me.

I was selfish, and selfish I remain.

I wanted Russell to go first. I knew how it would hurt her and I wanted it anyway. I knew that she would find a way to take it and he could not. He couldn't have lived for one minute in the pain losing her would have caused him. I am right about that. Folks thought he was the strong one. They were wrong.

It was always Mary.

Mary found a way to be strong without being tough. I wish I knew how. In Montgomery, at the height of the Civil Rights movement, Mary walked to the back of a city bus and sat down behind the line ignoring the boundaries that segregated folks in need of the same ride.

But she did so with grace.

She told me once of walking with her mother to listen to the radio broadcast announcing that Roosevelt was her president. She said it was important to her mother to hear it, and not having a radio, they had to walk to a friend's to listen. Years later at a dinner party Russell only hosted to try and convince me that he was the better cook, he told us a story about Mary's political convictions, a story I have repeated many times. They were the guests at a party given in their honor by the dean of Lenoir Rhyne, and the house was full of professors and scholars and academics. The host asked Russell why, after a lifetime of travel and living all over the world, they would choose to come back to Catawba County, North Carolina—back to Claremont. Before Russell could give the acceptable and understandable answer that they wanted to be near family, and in particular Mary's sister, he heard the soft and quiet voice of his wife answer,

"So we could *personally* vote against Senator Helms."

Yes, Mary was always the strong one.

I sat with her while Russell had heart surgery. We had worked it all out. Russell decided it would be too hard on Mary to spend the day in a waiting room of the hospital, so I was to stay at the house and keep her busy, and Gaye Morrison was to come to get her that evening and take her to see Russell when the worst was over, when he was fully awake and the sight of him wouldn't scare her. I chose *To Kill A Mockingbird*, went armed with the movie because Mary had just finished re-reading the book. I can hear her laugh—she had a good laugh—at the children when Scout climbed inside a tire and Jem and Dill rolled her so fast she got away from them and crashed into Boo Radley's porch. Mary said, "Those sweet children," when they stood in the balcony of the courthouse with a community of people whose only way of showing their respect and gratitude was to stand as Atticus Finch walked away from his losing effort to try and save one of those Mockingbirds. Mary cried with me when the light shone on the face of a man with shy ways who had saved the very children he loved to watch from the darkness of his windows, and when Scout said, "Hey Boo," Mary said. "Bless her heart."

When that movie was over, and we had laughed together and cried together and talked of the South and our love for it, and our disappointment when it has failed to live up to the songs of its better angels, Mary said, "Well, I have so enjoyed this, Shari. I am grateful to you for bringing the movie to me. I will always think of you when I see the book on my bookshelf and I would like to see Russell now."

It was not a request.

My suggestion that we wait until they called us was made to Mary's back. She was gathering her purse "and things" for her trip to the hospital. I called Gaye and said, "Look, Mary wants to go and she wants to go now, right now. You best be comin' to get her. She doesn't mean to wait." Gaye told me that she would have to clean up from the garden and that it would take her a good bit before she could be ready. She said to tell Mary to just hold on for a little while.

"*You* tell her," I said.

Gaye pulled up in the driveway without the bath she wanted to take and if you think that makes us both cowards, you are right.

Mary told us their love story one Christmas Eve as we gathered around their tree, how she had been engaged to another and gave back the ring when Russell came to call with roses picked from his mother's garden. She said that Russell told her that if she broke off her engagement, he very much wanted to see her, and Mary said that she would do exactly that but that her intended's father had just died, and she didn't want to hurt him so soon after. Russell asked her how long she needed to wait.

And there in the glow of the Christmas lights and the elegant decorations we had worked as a town to give to them, in the warmth of their home and the season of peace, Mary told us, "I thought two weeks was enough."

When, as a town, we read one book, *Ava's Man*, they read to one another. Russell would read to Mary. Mary would read to Russell. Terry flew in for a visit, and told me that he saw them there, waiting in the baggage claim, sitting next to one another, reading. He slipped into the chair next to them to listen to his mother read to his father, and it took them a few pages to realize he was there.

That scene plays in my mind when I think of them, surrounded by the noise and the chaos of an airport, people angry over lost bags or late flights, sad and crying in their goodbyes to loved ones, signs and balloons welcoming others upon arrival. But Russell and Mary, in their dignity and their grace and their never-ending love, read to one another, unaware of any of it, including their own beloved son who got to be there, right there, in it, to see it, to hear it, to feel it, but not be *of* it, for that was only for the two of them.

At the end of the story she told that Christmas, Mary said, "And I have been in love with him every day since."

I saw Mary this fall. I was selfish all over again. I just wanted her to go to Russell.

I am not sorry on this day, this day we say goodbye to Mary Boggs. I am only grateful. I am grateful for her bravery, a young white woman sitting at the back of a bus. I am grateful for her grace in battle, referring to political opposition as "Senator" even as she politely, with her hands folded in her lap, let strangers know she did not hold with his views of division and exclusion. I am grateful for her love of books and art and flowers and beauty in all forms and for the work she did alongside her husband to bring more of it to our community, when others believed we were less deserving of it than those big city folks. I am grateful to have seen unending courtesy and good Southern manners.

I am grateful to have seen true love.

And in my selfishness, I am grateful that it's over, that she doesn't have to spend another minute without him, that she doesn't have to wonder where he went because he is right there, as I am sure he always, always was. I know this is a loss for her children and her grandchildren and for every generation that has come, and will come, from this perfect love, that will walk this earth because of a perfect, perfect love; but all I can feel is grateful that it is as it should be, Russell and Mary Boggs, in love from the day of roses from a Carolina garden, and every day since.

THE LAST OF THEM
TO QUIT

He is the last of them to quit.

When I came to Claremont, Margaret Garrison was the principal of the elementary school. Peggy Miller served on every committee in town. Sometimes we made up committees just to get her to join and bake us a pound cake. Jerry Hoke fried our cheeseburgers and never said a word.

Except to me. He always talked to me.

In the Claremont Café Miss Janie took our money at the end of the line, putting the coins in a plastic butter tub wrapped in duct tape. I fear that might could be what started all this changing, replacing that butter tub with a divided drawer, though when I complained about it at the time she defended the decision by telling me, "We modernized." Russell and Mary Boggs hosted fancy dinner parties and garden parties and brought musicals to town. P.J. Stanley saved the world from the raging waters brought in by hurricanes named according to alphabet letters, and taught others how to behave in the face of devastation, which bandage to use, which way to run.

The Mayor was the The Mayor and The Chief was The Chief.

I suspect that the list of the important days of my life in Claremont is much different for me than for others. I hear them, like songs, rather than having them stuck with Scotch tape to scrapbook pages of memory in my head. It's always been that way. I can't really explain it, or maybe I don't want to. But I like it that way. I hear the sounds of the cars and Margaret welcoming her students on the Wednesday morning after 9/11, her voice, that voice, reminding them that this day was just like every day at Claremont Elementary, her peaceful kingdom, where they were safe and loved and though the world had changed all around us, they could count on Miss Garrison opening the door and saying, "Good morning, Walker. I hope you have a good day today. Do your best. I know that you will."

At Main and Lookout, The Chief would be getting out of his car, walking into the police station. In a little while, he would go to Hannah's Barbeque and they'll all talk about the tragedy and make more sense of it than anything being said on the television.

I can hear Miss Peggy talking to Shirley Harwell as they set the tables for our "Dinner with the Author," when Rick Bragg and Sonny Brewer came to town for the fifth anniversary of our library. Miss Peggy had asked me if I would ever get married again or just go on sinning as I was known to do. I asked her right back if *she* would marry again, and she said she certainly would not. Shirley said she didn't suppose she would either. Miss Peggy said it was too much work. "I can't take care of another man," she said. "My knees cannot take it."

That was a good day.

Laughing is how I remember The Chief. Rick was funny. Lord, he was funny that night. I can see The Chief, looking around the table and shaking his head, laughing harder than most everybody except Tony Garrison, who summed up the months of reading and work and the selling of the tickets and the publicity and the decorations and the food and cleanup with, "That was good."

Any time I walked into The Chief's office and said, "Hey, I've got an idea." He said, "How can we help ye?"

That's the song that plays when I think of The Chief. "How can we help ye?"

When I threw a hissy fit because they didn't give Avery an award for his Christmas display and threatened to Occupy Claremont if he wasn't given a proclamation for the ornamentation of the most festive lawn in this entire town, The Chief and his staff showed up to see him get it. I remember, because Miss Janie saw the crowd gathering in The Café and looked up at me over those glasses and said, "You've done it now. Somebody could rob the town blind and we'd never know it. Everybody's come to see Avery get his due."

Now think about that for just one moment. Our police chief came to see the guy who sweeps the floor get an award for decorating his yard.

When Mary Boggs came home from a long stay in the hospital, The Chief let me tie giant yellow ribbons all along Main Street to let her know how much we missed her. Russell pointed them out to her as they drove into town. When Russell and I wanted to throw a Bluegrass Festival on my lawn using my porch as a stage, The Chief blocked off two streets and gave us permission for Jeff Murray to drive his tractor and wagon around and around, giving rides to folks who wanted them, which was mostly the kids.

When Russell and Mary left for Texas, they got a police escort out of town. We stood along Depot Street, waving, crying, and watching them go. The Chief saw to it they left in style. I hear that, too—the people of Claremont, my people, hollering, "Goodbye Russell. Goodbye Mary. We love you. Come back."

And when they brought him back, my memory switches to pictures, flashes of what I could bear to take in, not his casket, not his family, not The Mayor, who couldn't hold himself upright from the loss, but it is The Chief I watched, standing at the back of the church making sure that all of Russell's instructions, his final time to boss us around real good, were carried out to the letter. Later, The Chief said to me that he was sorry he didn't get to hear all of what I read at the funeral, but he had to tend to the procession.

I knew he was there.

Two Decembers ago, when Shelly Miller and Roxanne Moser and I had a little more Christmas cheer than we might should have before going to the parade, Shelly said we needed not to take our pretty little snowman cups full of the Christmas spirit that had filled our hearts with joy. She said we would surely run into the Claremont police in the two blocks it took to walk from my house to Main Street. Roxanne took the cigarette from her mouth. "Naw, it's fine," she said, blowing smoke into the air. "We're with Shari. The Chief loves her."

I don't know if that's so or if he just got real good at dealing with drunks.

There is his favorite story of enlisting the help of the Official Town Drunk to run off some carpetbagger drunk who did not understand we got rules in Claremont as to who can and cannot lay around behind buildings to get sober. I have managed to get The Chief to tell that to every author I have brought to town. Just last November, he told it to one of the biggest hit songwriters in Nashville, who turned around and told it on stage in Austin, Texas two months later.

"Now folks, my friend Shari Smith is here tonight, and I know y'all read her writing cause I been talking about it all over my website and the Facebook and every word she writes is the truth. I just spent a few days in her town, and do you know that their Police Chief is so smart, he used a hometown drunk to run off a visitin' one?"

We're famous.

I think of all the kindness The Chief showed to Greg Issac, who absolutely knew how to make it hard to be kind to him. He belonged to us despite his shortcomings, and The Chief treated him like family, because he was family. And how many nights did Raymond not have to sleep in the cold because The Chief asked the nice people at the Super 8 to give him a room when the temperature dipped below the shelter a storage unit could provide.

What sort of grace does it take for a man in charge of law and order to overlook ordinances and bylaws and words on paper that don't serve the greater good, and decide instead to make sure a man is kept warm?

This is the story I tell of my town, of my Chief, a story of grace.

That music I hear, it includes The Chief laughing when my young'un and six of his best buddies discovered they were not cut out for a life of crime, as they couldn't even manage to steal Gantt Sigmon's chickens and dump them in the yard of their football coach without getting caught. What a sorry bunch of criminals they turned out to be, and they even had me as the mastermind.

I really thought I raised that boy better.

The Chief came when my house burned. The Chief came when tornado winds took roofs from their houses and spiked trees through walls. The Chief came when The Mayor and P.J. took a semi-truckload of Christmas trees to folks several states away, folks who had lost everything to a hurricane—everything but Christmas—which P.J. was not going to let happen. The Chief was there when Jason preached P.J. into the sky. I will hear the buzzing in my ears, the sound of trying to be numb, make the hurt go away when The Chief laid his hat on the box that held the dust of P.J. Stanley, the man born to do our unpleasant tasks.

I should have known it would fall to The Chief to pick up the slack.

He knew to laugh when teenagers steal chickens and cry when a good man goes into the clay, when to lock up a drunk and when to keep him warm, when to block off a street, and when to ignore the rules.

Margaret Garrison retired. Miss Peggy's health keeps her from her committee work. Miss Janie stepped out from behind the cash drawer at The Café and never went back. Jerry still comes in every day, sits at the Back Table, but it's not the same as having him behind the grill. The Mayor decided not to run, and Russell and Mary and P.J. are gone, all gone. Now, The Chief will hang up his badge. He is the last of them to quit.

The time of the Claremont I knew is gone and another time has taken its place. It's supposed to be that way, and I am mostly ready. I am. But, God, it was good. We got a library and we ran off the only person in this town who didn't like The Chief, and if you put a gun to my head and made me pick which one I am prouder of, I wouldn't be able to choose.

Alisa Carpenter and me put on a USO show and everybody came. We raised over ten thousand dollars for the library and then enlisted the help of her family and Kevin Isenhour to desecrate the holiday yard of a member of the city council and we didn't even go to jail. We turned Russell and Mary's house into a lovely picture postcard of Christmas in Williamsburg with greenery and fruit and perfect red bows, as the Abernathy boys vandalized Rita Busbee's yard with fornicating reindeer.

They didn't go to jail either.

Jerry started making birdhouses and talked to everybody, not just me. Well, not to everybody, but that's their own fault for being too sorry for him to bother with. We had scarecrow contests and Memorial Day services, and we rocked new babies, and we buried our dead when The Mayor was The Mayor and The Chief was the Chief.

Maybe The Chief isn't the last of them to quit. Maybe that falls to me. I didn't leave Claremont, only the two and a half square miles of land it sits upon. I took up with a guitar slinger from Texas and ended up in

Alabama with yet another family no kin to one another. I live on a river where moss hangs from the trees and boats drift past my kitchen window. I am in love, my children are happy, my grandchildren are perfect, a loyal German Shepherd dog lies at my feet as I end this story. Claremont lives in me and if I can tell it right, can capture that time, rusty in all the right places, it will live on the pages of a book yet to come.

As aggravated as some have been at me for not attending one of our five churches all those years, you can hardly blame me when you really think about it. You can understand my disbelief that I needed to get into heaven to see the angels. They walked the streets of my town every day. I called them by name. Margaret, Miss Peggy, Jerry and Janie, Russell and Mary, P.J..

And the Mayor was The Mayor and the Chief was The Chief.

ACKNOWLEDGEMENTS

Thank you, Robin Miura who insisted I should start a blog. Obstinance is my signature color. She was right and I was wrong. My sister-by-choice, Renee' Cannon, who littered her Facebook page with links to my stories I love you. Debbie Frazier is a constant reminder to pay better attention to the angels hovering near. No one lives the word "friend" more completely than Debbie.

To Claremont, the people who trusted me with their stories, there's a debt I can never repay. The Back Table Boys own a piece of my heart that is theirs alone, even the ones who are gone. They know that Jerry is my favorite and I have 149 birdhouses to prove that I am his favorite, too.

My love and undying gratitude goes to the authors who came to Claremont at my request; Rick Bragg, Sonny Brewer, Doug Crandell, Joe Formichella, Joe Galloway, Suzanne Hudson, Roger Pinkney, Carl T. Smith, and Baynard Woods,

To Chuck Cannon, another winged soul, thanks for writing the song I listen to, over and over, when I need to go where others fear to tread and for wanting to live there, in those rocky places of clarity. That is where you will find me.

To the Shoe Burners thank you for never giving in to more responsible notions that a steady paycheck is more important than art. May the gods of words and music shine their grace upon you, your songs, your stories, your souls.

Joe Formichella and Suzanne Hudson, thank you for Waterhole Branch, a soft place to fall, for taking away the commas I didn't need and reeling in sentences that didn't know when to stop running on. At least you got the comma thing right. Joe found the words that sent me to the page. I write because you could do that. No one else could.

Thank you to Courtney Spies for salvation at the beauty shop where redemption is stored between the blow dryers and the flat irons, and streaks of gray are sent straight to hell in a baptism of color by a chatty Yankee, an artist with a pair of scissors and a flat iron. You saved not only my hair but The Shoe Burnin'.

Judy Richards took on this book, shutting herself off from every thing and everyone else so that it could be. There are no words. All that comes to me is inadequate. Love is all I have for you.

Thank you to David Martin, for a list too long to fit in any book, for John David and Christen and Ava, and for Jill, very much for Jill, and...

To Laura Brooks for endless patience, for sharing when you shouldn't have to, for fine taste and good ears and for being fierce.

To my beloved friend Kerry, the most ethical person I know, who always tries no matter what.

To my beloved publisher Kerry, the most ethical person I know, who always tries no matter what.

To Randy Wilbourn and the entire team at Martin-Wilbourn Partners and River's Edge Media for talent and gifts writers and musicians don't possess, most especially Cary Smith for a cover that tells the story.

Thanks to the kind editors who bought my stories and mailed copies to my father and stepmother, Myrna. Thank you for giving my father a reason to keep breathing.

To Justin, who is more than a football player. Remember that.

To Nate and Abbie and Walker for allowing me the freedom to include your lives in my work and for bringing to the world around you all your goodness and light despite my failings.

To Matilda and Jack—I give you these stories so that you might know the family that came and went before you were born, better know the ones who welcomed you to this world, and forgive all the missteps we make trying to be half as perfect as you are.

And, to Chris, always my first reader. thank you for reminding me that before I am the organizer, the orchestrator, the momma and the bully I need to be to get our projects done, that I am first a writer, for knowing when to whisper that and when to holler, for playing your guitar while I write. I am better because of all that.

CPSIA information can be obtained at www.ICGtesting.com
Printed in the USA
LVOW11s0256240516

489678LV00003B/99/P